MY CORNISH WORLD

By the same author:

When Cornish Skies are Smiling
The Mill in the Valley
Family Circles
The Waterwheel Turns
Summer at the Mill
As the Stream Flows By
A Family at Sea
A View from the Valley
A Long Way to Land's End
A Family for All Seasons
All this and Cornwall Too
The Wind Blows from the West
Sunset over the Scillies
Spring at Land's End
The Petrified Mariner
An Old Mill by the Stream

Fiction:

Barbican's End
Rose
Karenza
A Work of Art
Martin's Cottage
At the Rainbow's End
The Girl in the Photograph
Thomasina's Island
The House on the Creek
Passenger to Penzance
At the Sea's Edge
The Secret Place
Echoes from the Cornish Cliffs
A Summer to Remember

My Cornish World

DENYS VAL BAKER

WILLIAM KIMBER · LONDON

First published in 1985 by
WILLIAM KIMBER & CO. LIMITED
100 Jermyn Street, London SW1Y 6EE

ISBN 0 7183 0545 0

Photoset in North Wales by
Derek Doyle & Associates Mold, Clwyd
and printed in Great Britain by
Biddles Limited, Guildford, Surrey

Contents

I

Wedding Days

Weddings and funerals are cornerstones of family life – unusual occasions at which all the scattered strands are drawn together and unfamiliar faces suddenly become familiar again. Recently I described the sad occasion of the funeral of my old friend Frank Baker and the gathering afterwards of his large family and circle of friends at a memorial service in St Hilary Church. Being an only child and with no relatives left except one or two remote cousins I seem to have escaped funerals in general but for Jess, part of a large family of five sisters and all their appendages, such occasions arise regularly. Now, sadly, one had come in the form of the funeral of her brother-in-law, Jim, married to her older sister Marjorie, and this meant a rather depressing journey up to Seaton on the Devon coast – where, of course, were gathered most of the members of the Bryan clan, including Jess's other sister, Frances, and her vicar brother-in-law, Degwell Thomas. Jim had been a nice jolly man, retired after a lifetime roaming the world as chief engineer on one of the big shipping lines – he will be greatly missed.

What Jess did not like to explain at the time was the rather ironic fact that the very next day she had to be back in Penzance to attend the very opposite sort of occasion – the wedding of our friend Jack Richards. Quite an unusual wedding in the circumstances for Jack was into his sixties, his bride still in her thirties – and she came all the way from

Turkey. And thereby hangs quite a story, much of it to do with the Val Bakers.

What happened was this. During one of our Mediterranean voyages in our old boat *Sanu* we had Jack as one of our passengers and he so much enjoyed the experience – cruising mostly around the Dodecanese Islands of Greece – that he made up his mind that this was the life for him. He would buy a boat and do some Med cruising for himself. So during much of our trip we constantly called in at boatyards in search of possible craft – Jack having decided in favour of one of the caiques favoured in the Eastern Mediterranean. At first he did not have much success but later on, after we had had to return home, Jack went to Turkey and there in the ancient port of Bodrum he found a boatyard that could build him just the boat he wanted – a 35-foot sailing caique with six berths and also room for a powerful diesel engine. During the next year Jack was constantly popping out to Bodrum to see how things were going on, and then after the boat was completed he decided to do some chartering which meant even more frequent visits to Bodrum.

It was during this time that Jess and her friend Beverly decided to take a Turkish holiday and stay with Jack on his boat – and it was the day after they arrived that Jack first confessed that he was becoming a little involved with a local Turkish lady, Filiz, but that he was gravely worried as to what to do because of the considerable age difference. As soon as Jess and Beverly met Filiz they found her delightful, a warm and lively creature who was obviously charmed by Jack and indeed ready and anxious to marry him.

'My dear Jack,' said Jess firmly, 'don't hesitate a moment longer. You have a wonderful chance of new happiness – don't let it slip by.'

Like a sensible chap Jack had finally taken the plunge, and now he and Filiz were in Cornwall and the great day had been fixed for the wedding – first a civil ceremony at St John's Hall, Penzance, and then a blessing service in a little church at

Towednack up near the Zennor moors. Along with Genevieve and little Megan, Jess and I went to St John's Hall – a little taken aback I suppose to find the ceremony taking place in what was normally the magistrate's court! In fact everything went off very well, and then we all got into our cars and drove over the moors to the very pretty little old church at Towednack.

Here was an unexpected hitch – the church was all locked up and there was no sign of the vicar. For over an hour we mooched around, beginning to get really cold in the February winds, until finally Jack's son by his earlier marriage, Michael, had the bright idea of driving quickly over to Zennor Church, which was also in the vicar's care. Sure enough that church was all lit up and warm and the vicar was sitting there awaiting his wedding party! At last the muddle was sorted out and soon we were all crowded into Towednack – though, alas, a very cold church.

Finally to the Queen's Hotel in Penzance for the elaborate reception and at last an opportunity to relax and greet many old friends – Anthony and Christianne Richards, Shirley Beck and her boy friend, Christopher, Eric Leaper and many others – among them members of the Richards family including an 89-year-old aunt who had travelled especially from Swansea, and who made a delightful impromptu speech wishing the bridal couple every happiness. Jess also made a humorous speech revealing how she and Beverly felt almost personally responsible for having brought about the happy occasion.

Finally – a charming Turkish custom apparently – Filiz went round the crowded room to thank every visitor personally with a ritual hug and a kiss. Altogether a very happy occasion, especially as two years ago Jack had been very seriously ill and indeed we hardly expected him to survive. Now, in his new bridegroom's suit with a white carnation and his face aglow with youthful happiness, he looked – well, just as a lucky bridegroom should look. And as for Filiz, she was radiant and equally happy. They were both looking forward to their plan to buy a caravanette and then drive slowly across Europe back to Bodrum, where they planned to settle down and lead an idyllic life.

Jack wasn't the only member of the Richards family whose wedding played a part in our family saga. More than twenty years previously, when we still lived at St Christopher's, our dear old home backing on to Porthmeor beach at St Ives, Jess and I had lent our 65-foot-long ground floor room (with glass doors opening on to the beach) for the wedding reception of Jack's son, Michael, when he married his Irish girl, Maureen. On that occasion the actual wedding took place in one of the local Methodist chapels at St Ives but I must say we enjoyed the reception rather more – one of those great St Ives' occasions with about a hundred guests and a liberal supply of wines and champagne. I can't remember now what time of the year it was, but no doubt if at the height of summer then many of us would have ended by donning bathing costumes and running out to have a surf in the great booming waves of Porthmeor.

There was no surfing on Mike and Maureen's honeymoon – but they did spend it with us, for our present to them was an invitation to come along with us on a cruise from St Ives across the English channel to Le Havre and then up the 250 miles of the River Seine which eventually brought us into the heart of Paris (we moored within a stone's throw of the Champs Elysées). I am sure Mike and Maureen have never forgotten that marvellous experience, culminating, at the Paris end of things, with the four of us strolling past Notre Dame and finding an intimate red table-clothed restaurant by the edge of the river where we dined and wined and ended up dancing with the manager and other diners to the strains of an accordion. Afterwards a taxi back to Port de Plaisance and then we all leaned over a bridge looking down on the waters of the Seine now sparkling with reflected lights – and there, below us, the warm and friendly glow from the gaslit saloon of dear old *Sanu*. These are not the sort of moments one forgets.

Michael in particular will also remember a later stage of our trip back down the Seine! As dusk approached we decided to pull in behind a row of barges waiting for the morning opening of the next lock. On this occasion Mike was at the wheel so I went forward with a rope ready to jump ashore. As *Sanu* glided closer to the bank I stood idly waiting, watching the rear of the nearest steel barge coming nearer, waiting meanwhile for Mike to put *Sanu* into reverse.

I waited ... and waited ... and suddenly with a terrifying jerk *Sanu* seemed to leap forward and crashed straight into the back of the barge! The moment is etched into my mind: I could not believe my eyes. What happened of course was something which happened several times to myself – in a state of momentary confusion, Mike put the gear forward instead of into reverse, and by the time he corrected the mistake it was too late.

The next few moments were quite comic. The crew of the barge had been asleep – now they came rushing on deck, gesticulating and making anguished movements of their hands. Mike and I stood there apologising profusely in English, which wasn't very effective as they obviously only spoke French. At last when they had calmed down a little the skipper demanded that we accompany him to make an official report to the lock-keeper. Between us we had to fill up four or five official forms, including lengthy details of our boat and what had happened.

By the time this was all over Mike and I crawled back exhausted. Even then we had had to promise that one of us would be available at six in the morning for an official measurement of the damaged parts of the barge. Mike took on this task and later when we came down to breakfast we found him rather dazed – apparently the occasion had been token rather than of real importance, and they had all ended up sitting down at the lock keeper's office drinking whisky together.

Mike and Maureen were not actually joined in holy matrimony aboard *Sanu*, but this event too is included in my dossier of weddings, for in fact while cruising around Ithaca, one of the Ionian Isles, my son Stephen and his American girl, Gina, were married aboard *Sanu* – by me, the captain. I had always had the vague idea that ship's captain *could* perform such a ceremony, but now I began to wonder just how much of a ship's captain one had to be for the proceedings to be legal. Buried deep in the heart of fabled Ithaca it seemed impossible for me to check up on such a fine point. After some hesitation I decided that since Stephen and Gina seemed very much in love, and could always get married more officially on their return to 'civilization', there didn't seem any harm in going through with what in fact proved to be a touchingly beautiful ceremony.

Naturally everyone aboard *Sanu* was soon geared up for such a special occasion. The first item to be decided was the venue for the wedding. Port Vathy we felt to be a little too normal and official. What we wanted was a completely deserted stretch of coastline, far from the madding crowd. According to the rules of general maritime law, I think we should have been well out at sea, but that would have been practically impossible in an area bounded by so many islands: so we chose, as the next best thing, an incredibly beautiful cove known as Pera Pigadhi, off the eastern tip of Ithaca.

I often think back to *Sanu*'s slow approach to Pera Pigadhi, at about four o'clock on a shimmering July afternoon. The coastline consisted of a series of rearing mountain cliffs broken here and there by a thin valley – then at last we saw the cove we were aiming for, the water so deep that we had to go quite close in to be able to anchor, even then in depths of forty feet. The water was absolutely glassy, we could see the bottom quite clearly – ahead of us a white sandy beach, all around tall cliffs covered with heather. It was an idyllic spot, most suitable for an idyllic event.

Such occasions, however, require careful planning. Genny and Llewelyn (son of our friends Frank and Kate Baker) had volunteered to see to the catering side, and apart from preparing a meal for later on in the evening Genny had whipped up a wedding cake on which Llew had executed a complicated floral design worthy of an ex-student of Falmouth Art School. For liquid refreshments we had bought three large bottles of the Greek equivalent of Asti-Spumante, and they had been cooling off all day. Next there was the question of the bride and groom's attire. We had not exactly come out to Greece with a vast selection of clothes: what we had were mostly summertime shirts and shorts, that sort of thing – so some kind of improvisation was necessary.

In the end Stephen appeared in white jeans and open shirt, with a bright red sash wound round his waist – Gina, more decoratively, was ensconced in an extraordinary combination of some sort of petticoat covered with an enormous length of muslin which Jess had brought on the boat as a mosquito net for spreading over our bed every night – but which now gave just the right wedding-day touch. A piece of this was also torn off and used to attire little Nell, Llew's daughter, who was the official bridesmaid, her father being the best man. Finally, as the officiating officer in the ceremony, I wore my best summer suit crowned by an enormous Spanish sombrero which happened to have been left on the boat from a previous trip.

By six o'clock all was ready. The sun, which had been almost unbearably hot, had just mercifully sunk behind one of the taller mountains, leaving us with a pleasant cool evening light. *Sanu* wafted gently at her mooring, not a ripple disturbing the sea: everywhere there was hush and beauty, warmth and affection. Up in the bow of the boat I stood in readiness, my sombrero pushed back to give me a better view of the proceedings. It was a long time since my own ceremony twenty-five years ago when Jess and I were married at South Kensington Registrar's Office – and I had a rather dim memory of the spoken lines, but fortunately Frank and Kate were a little more accurate in their remembrance of such things past. Between us we had had one or two 'run throughs' and managed to produce a fairly reasonable sequence of rhetorical questions. 'Do you Stephen Val Baker take this woman Gina Brown to be your lawful wedded wife ... in sickness and in health ... etc., etc.?'

Beforehand I had been inclined to be a little jittery about the whole thing, more than once wishing fervently I had never agreed to Stephen's request. In the event, perhaps not altogether surprisingly in the face of all that beauty around, all that affection aboard, the ceremony not only passed off without a technical hitch, but was curiously moving. After I had read out the basic marriage vows and Gina and Stephen had repeated them after me slowly and clearly, Llew had produced not one but two rings, which the bridal couple laughingly exchanged: then Kate – a former Shakespearean actress – stood up and in a lovely resonant voice recited one of Shakespeare's famous love sonnets.

As the last cadence of her voice died away on the fragrant early evening air, that was the signal for boisterous congratulations, everyone kissing everyone else, three cheers for the bride and groom. Out came the three carefully guarded bottles of sparkling wine, glasses appeared, and we all drank long and lasting toasts to the happiness of the slightly abashed Stephen and Gina.

Responding to the spirit of the occasion Stephen and Gina then threw off their wedding clothes and dived over the side of the boat into that marvellous warm sea, and swam over to the shore ... there to sit, leaning against a rock, staring dreamingly into their own private future.

I have failed miserably, I see at once, to capture the strange atmosphere of my one and only marriage at sea ... because, I suppose, the things that I seek to capture can hardly be pinned down to paper. Beforehand, as I say, I had some misgivings: what had begun almost too lightly, not as a joke exactly, but in something in the spirit of good humour, might easily have proved a fiasco. To all our reliefs, this was not so. For Stephen and Gina, obviously, this essentially private ceremony, carried out in such a beautiful setting, among loving friends, did acquire a meaning and significance quite beyond its dubious legal status. At the end of it all, undoubtedly, they *felt* married, which is really all that matters. For us who had shared in the simple proceedings there was a lesson in age old ordinary wisdom: it is not so much the way you do a thing that matters, what matters is *why* you do it. If Stephen and Gina had not been in love, then the ceremony would have been meaningless and unworthy. As it was they cared and we cared – and so they were married.

Certainly no one could have asked for a more beautiful setting for a wedding, official or otherwise. Long after the light had vanished that night we stayed on deck under a magical starlit sky, marvelling at our good fortune to be here in Ithaca, perhaps along with Odysseus and all his Nymphs! It was very late before we finally went to bed – after one of the most memorable days not merely of our trip, but of our lives.

Most of the weddings we have attended seem to have taken place in Penzance – in the old days in a very antiquated office with peeling wallpaper, a most depressing setting. It appeared particularly depressing, I remember, on the occasion of a somewhat unusual ceremony between a friend of ours and a man from overseas. This was no love match but what might fairly be called a marriage of convenience – the foreigner's permit to stay in England had run out but if he married an English girl he could remain. Our friend was fancy free and friendly with him so she offered to become his wife and so enable him to stay on – alas, the false nature of the ceremony somehow came through and we found it difficult to raise much cheer. Ironically enough in later years there was much acrimony between the couple, even though they never lived together, and altogether this is one form of marriage I would not recommend.

Our own children's marriages, on the other hand, have been very happy occasions. Apart from Stephen, Gill and Jane are both married, and have been for many, many years. Gill and Alan were married at Kingston Registry Office and held their reception party in the lush garden of my mother's old house in Surbiton. Jane's marriage to Rick was an altogether more elaborate affair, a ceremony at Wandsworth Registry Office and then a big reception at Jane's flat in Putney. As for the other half of our family of six children – well they have all had their opportunities and plenty of fruitful relationships, but so far not got around to that final binding together. In another chapter I describe something of Demelza's love life – meantime it is to our oldest, Martin, and our youngest, Genevieve, that Jess and I still look hopefully to provide us with yet another excuse for those most pleasant of occasions, more wedding parties.

II

Long Live The Public Lending Right!

For authors like myself 1984 had indeed been a red letter year for it saw the introduction at long last of the long awaited Public Lending Right scheme, under which authors henceforth receive what is politely described as a small fee (actually 1.02p!) every time one of their books is borrowed from a public library. Considering that ever since public libraries came into existence in the last century books have been available free, and further that the annual loaning out figure is an astounding 648,622,000 copies, it does seem more than a little appropriate that the mere author should be allowed to share, however sparsely, in this bonanza. After all for every solitary copy of our book in a library, who knows, there may be as many as 50 lost sales to members of the public, many of them potentially buyers.

Not surprisingly authors (myself among them) have been grumbling at the unfairness of this position for many decades past. Indeed they have done more than bemoan; through their representative bodies the Society of Authors and the Writers Guild they have been in the forefront of the battle to bring about a change. What has been surprising, to me at any rate, is that our biggest antagonists in this battle were none other than the librarians – despite the self-evident fact that without us authors they would have no livelihoods! Indeed the nearer we got to achieving public lending right the shriller and fiercer became the opposition, with stirring talk about last-ditch stands on a matter of principle, and so on and so forth. The matter of principle was in fact a valid one – it was felt to be almost a sacred credo that the public should have the right to borrow books *freely*. However there were many times, as I struggled with one financial hardship after another, when I could not help wishing a thought or two might be spared for the mere author rather than his free reader. Never mind, all has ended in a sensible compromise – the public still get their books free and the government has allocated a special fund of £2,000,000 to cover the new Public Lending Right Act – less 'administrative costs' which reduces it to £1,588,000, but let's accept that with good humour since at least there's still over one and a half million left to be shared out among 6,000 authors.

The Public Lending Right Act which finally won its way to parliamentary approval was, needless to say, hardly in the exact shape we authors had originally proposed, but we must be thankful for small mercies. For instance the figure of 1.02 pence per book borrowed appears to me to be so ludicrously low as to be comtemptible – surely 5p would have been more reasonable? Still, there it is. As for the way the scheme is operated – well it sounds a little complicated but I suppose in the circumstances is fair enough. What happens is that an estimate is arrived at of the number of times each library book is borrowed on a nationwide basis. Obviously there would be neither time nor labour available to carry out this work in every library so what has been done is to choose 16 sample libraries, (two in Wales, two in Scotland, two in Northern Ireland, three in the North of England, three in the South of England, two in the Metropolitan boroughs and two in London). As far as possible these 16 libraries are chosen due to their representative nature and all borrowings from these are recorded on a computer: finally this figure is multiplied to arrive at a figure based on the actual loans from all public libraries.

In their first official report the Public Lending Right

Authority has given some interesting financial figures. For instance, in theory no less than £270,000 should have gone to just a few best-seller authors – however thanks to a sensible provision that no author can earn more than £5,000 this means that the 'loot' has been spread around more equitably. Payments to authors earning PLR in the first year of the scheme's operation averaged £261, and the number of authors in various payment categories were as follows: 46 authors received the maximum of £5,000, 81 authors got between £2,500 and £4,999, 247 between £1,000 and £2,499, 318 between £500 and £999, 1516 between £100 and £499, and 3,878 less than £99. Unfortunately, money having lost its value so drastically, these figures are not all that encouraging. *If only* it *had* been 5p a book! – then we would have really been into meaningful sums like £25,000, £12,500 and so forth.

Listening to a BBC book programme organised by Hunter Davies I was hardly surprised to learn that the full figure had been earned by such best-sellers as Barbara Cartland and Jeffrey Archer. I was, however, a little taken aback to learn that some very well-known writers were down in the few hundreds. So yes, obviously, it is all a bit of a lottery.

When news of the scheme first being accepted first came out I felt no immediate personal interest. I presumed that my books would return a high figure if a return was made by a Cornish library, but this seemed most unlikely. Consequently when my son Martin asked me what sort of return I expected I shook my head despondently.

'I suppose if I'm lucky – maybe two or three hundred.'

Martin gave a mysterious smile.

'You're wrong there. Your books are in all the libraries up country. Just you wait and see. I'll have a bet with you – you'll get at least a thousand, probably much more.'

I appreciated Martin's loyalty but went on shaking my head for many more months. And then one bright day in January the PLR computer statement for my books arrived – and I had quite a few surprises as I stared at the first and most important column, 'National Loans'.

The first surprise was that it was my novels and short stories that had been in most demand, rather than my autobiographies. The second pleasant surprise were the figures themselves. For instance my novel *Rose* had been borrowed nationally no less than 21,533 times – similarly my novel *Barbican's End* (my favourite) had been borrowed 20,397 times. Among other fiction work, a book of short stories called *The House on the Creek* had been borrowed 20,240 times, another book of stories called *Passenger to Penzance* had been borrowed 15,976 times, while other books of stories – *Thomasina's Island* and *At the Sea's Edge* – returned figures of 11,477 and 14,548 respectively.

Among the autobiographies the figures were as follows: *A Family for All Seasons*, 15,172; *A Long Way to Land's End*, 11,935; *Summer at the Mill*, 11,034; *An Old Mill by the Stream*, 7,608; *All This and Cornwall, Too*, 9,122; *A Family at Sea*, 7,869; *Upstream at the Mill*, 6,740; *A View from the Valley*, 5,321; *The Wind Blows from the West*, 6,435; and *The Waterwheel Turns*, 6,581.

Altogether the borrowings came to a grand total of just over a quarter of a million – a factor I am still trying to take in fully. After all, it's quite a thought. So many people, so many readers – who are they all? Where are they all? What kind of people are they? I'd love to know, but I suppose I never shall. All the same it does give an author a genuinely warm feeling to learn that a real form of communication exists. Of course, if that quarter of a million borrowers had been a quarter of a million purchasers – well, yes, indeed, I could buy a luxury yacht and start cruising the world all over again ...

But far be it from me to complain.

'There you are, dad,' said my son Martin. 'What did I tell you? You're more than a couple of thousand better off.'

'Indeed I am,' I replied cheerfully. Then, prompted by some instinct I looked down among the PLR information notes, and gave a small groan.

'But guess what – I still have to pay tax on it!'

And in due course I was to learn even worse – because I was now an old age pensioner and allowed to earn only a limited amount above my pension the acquisition of this new money could well result, in fact, in most of my pension being cut down. So alas, as so often, I was to find that as the Government gives with one hand so it takes away again with the other.

Still, it's nice to get a little acknowledgement!

*

Upon reflection, having written at some length about an author's point of view, it seems only fair to give the librarians some space, and I cannot do better here than outline some of the achievements of our own excellent Cornwall County Library Service. There is now a network of 20 branch libraries, large and small, throughout the county. Each provides a lending service to children and adults, a reference and information service and is an agent for the central services of the library. The libraries vary in size considerably and the very small branches, such as Camelford and Padstow, hold only very limited stocks of books, and are open usually on only three days each week. However, these are linked with a large library and there is a constant interchange of book-stock, between the large and the small, in an endeavour to keep the stocks alive and interesting. The small libraries usually have a quick-reference section, but this is augmented by the much wider selection in the larger libraries which are available as information centres by telephone or letter. The services of the branch libraries are available to all the local population, whether or not they actually live in the towns, and many country people use the branch libraries when they pay their weekly or fortnightly visit to the local market town.

The second source of supply for the countryman is through his travelling library. There is now a fleet of nine vehicles, each based on the largest library in the district, and these penetrate to the most isolated parts of the county. It is not possible to visit individual houses, but all villages, and most groups of houses and cottages receive a fortnightly, and in some cases weekly call from the travelling library. We are fortunate in Cornwall in that the winters are never really very severe, and the service is able to run unhindered by bad weather, winter and summer alike, except for the occasional mechanical breakdown. Each travelling library carries a stock of between 1,800 and 2,000 volumes of adult books, but does not cater for children except with a very limited selection of books for the pre-school child. Each vehicle has a circulating stock of approximately 8,000/10,000 volumes, plus, of course, the stock of the district library from which it operates.

The 'special' services are those administered centrally from County Library headquarters at County Hall. A purpose-built library was completed on the eve of the outbreak of the Second World War, and occupied by the library until when the new County Hall was completed a larger building became vacant, and the rapidly expanding library service was moved into this, its present home. This now houses the Central Lending Library, the Music and Drama Library, Cornish Collection and the administrative offices. The Schools Library Service and the central book store are unfortunately still in separate buildings.

The Drama Library consists of a collection of sets of plays and many single copies, together with a selection of books on the theatre, the production of plays, and acting. A catalogue is published from time to time, and is available through the branch libraries. The plays are issued to dramatic societies and schools for reading and selection, but not for production purposes. During recent years the collection has received a major overhaul and is now well-equipped to meet most of the demands placed upon it.

The Gramophone Record Library is a recent additional service offered by the County Library and the collection of records now covers the main works in the classical repertoire. There are printed catalogues available for sale at all branch libraries, and these list the full collection of over 2,000 discs.

The records are available on a request system through all branch libraries and the Headquarters' library. They are also available to residents of Truro City and Camborne-Redruth by co-operative agreement.

The library of sheet music has never been very fully developed, and the present collection is very restricted, although efforts are now being made to improve the service, and the Music Librarian is currently engaged in producing a list of piano scores held at the Central Library. By agreement, through the South-West Regional Library Bureau, Plymouth City Music Library allows its stock to be used, and a great amount of sheet music is available on request. It is hoped that this side of the library's activities will expand considerably in future, to meet the undoubted need in Cornwall.

The study of local history is always strong in any county, but in Cornwall, because of the richness of its flora, fauna, the geology, unique history, and industrial background, it takes precedence over many other popular studies. There is a rich fund of published material on Cornwall, perhaps more than for many other counties, and the County Library has bought judiciously in this area for many years, with the result that there is now a very fine reference collection in the Headquarters' Library at the old County Hall, which is open to students during normal office hours. Postal enquiries on Cornish questions are constantly received at this Library from many parts of the United Kingdom and abroad, particularly from the USA and Australia. A significant addition to the Cornish Collection was made in 1965, when the private library of the late Mr Ashley Rowe was purchased for the County Library. In addition to the central reference collection, Cornish material is added to the stocks of all the branch libraries, and a special effort is being made to build up reasonably comprehensive collections in the seven Regional libraries. Good collections already exist in Liskeard, Launceston and St Ives, and adequate study facilities are available.

The coverage of Reference Material poses a major problem in a county like Cornwall, as with twenty branch libraries, and nine travelling libraries the book resources of the service are spread very thinly, and even then there are considerable distances between branch libraries. It is obvious that on economic grounds one cannot provide a really good reference collection at all service points, and there is therefore a three-tier system for information requests. Each small sub-branch library has a 'quick-reference' selection, usually no more than a few shelves of books, but capable of providing answers to a fairly wide range of basic questions, these represent the bottom tier of the pyramid. The second or middle tier of provision is through the seven 'regional' libraries at Bodmin, Helston, Launceston, Liskeard, Newquay, St Austell and St Ives, where every effort is made to provide a good range of the standard reference books, and up-to-date key yearbooks and directories. At these libraries there is usually a qualified librarian available on the premises, to help enquirers with their more difficult questions. A great deal of very useful information is readily available from the reference stocks of these libraries, and, of course, they are all on the telephone and the librarians can answer or record verbal enquiries. The peak of the pyramid is the headquarters' library at Truro, where the County Reference Librarian and his staff have a much wider range of books and resources available to deal with highly complicated enquiries. Naturally this cannot be compared with the technical and commercial enquiries systems operated by large urban library authorities, but it is true to say that very few enquiries go unanswered.

An interesting development in reference and information work is the establishment of the Cornwall Technical Information Service, centred on the Library of the Cornwall Technical College, but working through the main branches of the County Library, and the four independent library authorities in West Cornwall. This information service is offered to industry, commerce, the professions and individuals throughout Cornwall who have an information problem. Requests for information which cannot be satisfied at local branch library level are channelled up through the County Reference Librarian, and those not cleared from County Library resources are then passed to the College Librarian. Many highly complex questions have been dealt with successfully, and it is hoped that commercial and industrial interests will make increasing use of the service.

The fourth major service offered by the County Library is the Schools Library Service, financed by the Education Committee and freely available to all LEA schools. Through this service every school, infant, primary, secondary, grammar and comprehensive, receives a supply of books for the school library. In the infant and primary schools, the County Library supplies the entire stock, and this is exchanged or part-exchanged normally every term. Books for the exchanges are selected from the shelves of the Schools Mobile Library by the School staff with help from a librarian who travels with the vehicle. The secondary schools, secondary-modern, comprehensive and grammar, all have funds for library books which they spend, either independently, or through the Schools Library Service, and these collections are renewed and improved by the County Schools Librarian on her regular visits to them. Great care is exercised in the selection of book stock for the schools, and a permanent exhibition of recommended books is on display at the Schools' Library Service Headquarters at old County Hall, Truro. The service co-operates very closely with the School Library Association, and the librarian is always prepared to advise head teachers or school librarians on library topics. The great merit of the scheme is that children who live in remote areas throughout the county have access to books, even though they may be unable to use the nearest branch library.

This brief survey shows what has been achieved, and how the service stands at present. Much remains to be done in the county to give all residents access to a full library service suited to the needs of the second half of the twentieth century. As indicated earlier, the Library Committee is aware of the problems and has formulated plans for development. In the words of Cornwall's County Librarian: 'There are many interesting and exciting possibilities under discussion, and it is hoped that in future the qualified staff will be able to take a more positive part in serving local communities by initiating direct contact with people who have a need for the services which a modern library can offer. In an age of growing concern for education in its broadest sense, the library service has a unique contribution to offer, and is seen by those who work in it as one of the institutions which, properly used, can lead to an enrichment of life for the individual and the community.'

III

'Demelza's Baby'

One evening in March we all sat around a television set watching a programme in the BBC's *Forty Minutes* series. It was called 'Demelza's Baby' and it told the story of how, after becoming pregnant and deciding to have her baby, Demelza and her close woman friend, Judy, were coping with the problems of forming a family unit and bringing up Morgan, as the new arrival was known.

Described in the *Radio Times* as 'one of the most unusual and fascinating of love stories', 'Demelza's Baby' had already, understandably, aroused considerable controversy, and was to continue to do so for quite a while. It was, however, no flash in the pan affair but something that had germinated and developed over quite a period of time – at least a year, I fancy. In the very beginning Demelza and Judy had often wondered about adopting a baby and creating a little family unit of their own, but somehow the idea never seemed quite right. They wanted a child that would really be theirs, really belong to them – sometimes, half jokingly and half in earnest, they would imagine Demelza becoming a real mother.

Then during a summer tour with her Afro-rock band, Zambula, Demelza found herself in the situation of spending a night with a member of the band she had always liked, though would never love. Soon afterwards she missed a period, and then another, and finally a visit to the doctor confirmed that she was pregnant.

Now the first of innumerable problems arose. Despite all their earlier (admittedly theoretical) discussions Judy became unhappy about what had happened and for a time the whole relationship, which had gone on for more than two years, seemed on the verge of breaking up. It might well have done but obviously there were strong bonds there somewhere – after a hectic few days the two girls made up their differences and decided to go ahead, turning what had been a theory into what was going to be a very definite fact. Suddenly, indeed, as we could see, they both became very excited like any other parents-to-be. Sad to say, though not surprisingly, this euphoria was soon to be shattered: as the news leaked out there were many criticisms not merely from conventional people but even from some of their feminist friends.

Judy and Demelza were hurt and dismayed and for a while retired into comparative seclusion. They even, in order to escape the endless discussions, went off for a short holiday in France and it was while over there, strolling by a leafy river bank one evening, that suddenly, and in my opinion rightly, they thought angrily, no, we won't let people get us down – it's going to be our baby and our family, and that's that.

It was at this point, after Demelza and Judy had returned to life in Penzance, that her older sister Jane came into the picture. Jane is a film editor at the BBC and had recently been appointed to the *Forty Minutes* series which was always on the look-out for controversial topics. Quite a feminist herself Jane felt angry at the way the girls had been criticised. In these more enlightened days what was wrong with two women companions choosing to bring up a child of their own? What indeed? Certainly there was a case to be made. Jane took the whole problem to Roger Mills the executive producer in charge of the *Forty Minutes* series – there were several high level discussions among various BBC departments – and at last the decision was made: Let's make a film – we'll call it 'Demelza's Baby'.

The BBC decision to make a film was one thing: getting

Demelza and Judy to agree – not surprisingly – was quite another. At first they were both adamant that they didn't want all the hustle and publicity; it was their own private affair and so forth. Jane would have none of that. 'You owe it to other women who might want to do the same but lack the courage to take the initiative ... ' There were comings and goings, first Jane on her own, then she came down a second time with Roger Mills to add a persuasive voice – finally she came yet again this time bringing with her the likable young Irishman who had been appointed to direct the film, Richard Lightbody. Perhaps his persuasive lilting Irish voice did the trick – at any rate after a lot of humming and hawing, Demelza and Judy agreed they would do the film.

All this had taken quite a time, a few weeks, even months, and in pregnancy time waits for no mother – suddenly our sylph-like daughter had ballooned out into a very fat young lady indeed. Jess and I couldn't help being amused as we saw Demelza regarding herself in the mirror in anguish. Fortunately, like all mothers-to-be, she acquired along with the plumpness a certain almost indefinable other quality. Demelza is rather beautiful anyway, and now that outer beauty was enhanced and liberated as we noticed on the many sunny afternoons when she would drive over to the Mill and then lie sunbathing on our lush green lawn, by the side of the gurgling mill stream. By this time Demelza and Judy had settled in a comfortable cottage over at Pendeen on the north coast, where they led a very domestic life and seemed very happy, but fortunately for us the Mill still had its attractions.

Now, some six months after the whole thing had been first mooted, the *Forty Minutes* team started seriously working on their film. Headed by the enthusiastic Richard the unit came down to stay in a Penzance hotel and arrange a few early sequences – Demelza and Judy walking on the cliffs and discussing their problems, Demelza and Judy buying wallpaper for the new nursery – then the two separately each being interviewed and encouraged to talk around all their problems

– finally one or two filling-in explanatory shots, like Demelza's visit to her gynaecologist and Judy shown working at the small café she runs in Penzance – and, of course, Demelza (a very large and pregnant Demelza!) still playing away on the congas with Zambula at their regular gigs at the Coastguard, Mousehole, and at Kenegie Manor at Gulval.

As is generally the case filming turned out to be a mixture of arduous hard work and unexpected pleasures. There were exasperating days when take after take was necessary on such mundane happenings as a simple shopping expedition in Penzance – but then there were more elevated days, as when the whole unit went to Porthcurno Cove or maybe out on to the great booming surfing beach at Sennen. On such occasions not merely the director and photographer and sound recordist were of importance – equally important was the general factotum, Paddy, who somehow, out of the wilds of the Logan Rock, could produce a dozen pasties and a crate of beer.

One of the nicest occasions from our point of view was one evening when it was decided to film Zambula playing out in the open on the big lawn outside Demelza's caravan in the grounds of our home. We had gathered together enough wood to build a huge bonfire and arranged a huge circle of seats around – now the band gathered with their instruments, singer Wendy launched into her regular opening song, 'Too Late', Tito, the Ugandan conga player began thumping out, soon to be joined by Demelza – and all at once the valley was indeed alive with the sound of music.

With her usual aplomb, Paddy arrived bearing a crate of white wine; there were salads and cheeses, altogether the makings of a really good party. And so it proved, only this one was being recorded as well, so that there was quite a footage for the eventual film, showing Zambula in a happy mood, and Demelza particularly alive and kicking (or perhaps I should say Morgan).

It was interesting watching the film unit at work. During the last three months of Demelza's pregnancy they made several trips down in order to record differing stages of the pregnancy. Each time I usually had a chat with Richard, the director, and was always impressed by his dedication – pleased, too, that he so obviously was determined to make an effective and persuasive film out of what could be a very difficult subject. Even so I was constantly surprised at the inconveniences he was prepared to subject himself and his companions – culminating in the plans for the actual birth time.

'We've all got these bleepers, you see, Denys, linked up with head office. As soon as Paddy gets word that Demelza has gone into labour she'll bleep us all, wherever we are, and – hey presto we'll be on our way down.'

And this is exactly what happened. About ten o'clock one evening in May, Judy rang up Paddy in London to tell her Demelza had started labour and she was about to drive her the 25 miles to Treliske Hospital, Truro. Paddy pressed all her bleeps and in various London suburbs Richard and his crew got the message, quickly gathered their equipment together – and started the long drive down to Cornwall ... When we arrived at Treliske at ten o'clock the next morning the first familiar faces we saw were Paddy and Richard, hanging around the hospital ward!

Jess and I had hoped to be present to see the actual birth but Demelza turned out to be a quick operator, and the new arrival was already out into the big worrying new world by the time we reached the ward. However the event had only just taken place, and so we were able to see a practically virgin bundle of wizened flesh and bone and blood – while Richard and his cameras were soon able to worm their way past the matron and get a few early shots of 'Demelza's Baby'. These included shots of a proud Judy standing by the bedside, as well as of both Jess and me rather gingerly cradling the new arrival in our arms.

Actually the baby's name had been decided long beforehand – Morgan – after Captain Morgan of the rum fame, since this was one of Demelza's favourite drinks. Somehow it seemed quite an apt name, especially after the wrinkles had smoothed out to reveal the rather handsome young gentleman – and oh so placid, such a contrast to his mother.

After a couple of days at Treliske, Demelza was transferred down to the Bolitho Maternity Home in Penzance, a much more satisfactory arrangement all round, both for us and for the film unit. Bolitho's is one of those nice easy-going, old-fashioned maternity homes where people can come and go almost at will, and over the next few days Demelza was able to entertain rather like royalty, being visited by a stream of friends and brothers and sisters, etc. She was, of course, by now feeding Morgan at the breast and with her own self now relaxed she looked really beautiful with that touch of the ethereal which women often seem to develop on such occasions.

All was honey and light at Bolitho's. Once Demelza and Judy and Morgan had returned home to Pendeen, however, life suddenly became much more difficult. Like any other mother Demelza felt a little lost and confused, confronted with one problem after another. However Judy turned out to be a tower of strength, taking over all the tasks possible and helping to make the new arrival feel really at home.

Some of this the film unit recorded, then they went away having arranged to come back in five months time to shoot some last sequences. When they did return they did a long sequence of Zambula playing a concert at Demelza's Ballroom, Penzance, and it was after this concert that we all gathered at a farewell party at the Regent Hotel, given by the film unit. Jane was down for this: she had already done quite a bit of editing on the film and was waxing enthusiastic.

'It's going to be all right, the film. It's a difficult subject but it's been handled most delicately – I'm very pleased.'

What Jane didn't mention was that she had been working endlessly long hours on what for her was a labour of love – a fact that was to be revealed when we finally saw the finished product.

We quite missed the film unit when they had gone for the last time. For a while there was a sense of anti-climax, especially as the showing of the film was put off for two or three months. Then finally a firm date was announced for March, only a few weeks away – and of course Demelza and Judy both began having second thoughts.

'Perhaps we shouldn't have done it. What will people think? Will we become outcasts?'

I must admit both Jess and I at times did wonder. People can be very cruel and hidebound – how would the local people react?

Above all, how would the millions of viewers react?

Fortunately we were able to have a foretaste, for up in London the BBC held a preview of the film for the press. Jane was there and reported back happily that everyone had appeared to be very impressed and even moved. Still, one could never be sure.

*

And so to the night itself. Jess and I drove to Pendeen and watched 'Demelza's Baby' with Demelza and Judy and Jane. From the moment of the title sequence, showing a dreamily pregnant Demelza wandering among the cliffs we were captivated – the film, it seemed to us, was very well made indeed, right down to the magnificently picturesque last shots showing Demelza and Judy walking arm in arm along Sennen beach against a background of huge white waves endlessly cascading over the sands. There was nothing offensive, nothing that jarred – instead one got a picture of a loving relationship that was obviously being cemented by the baby – the exact point which the film makers had wanted to get across.

We opened a bottle of champagne, and I made a toast.

'Here's to Morgan – here's to "Demelza's Baby".'

What's more, the next day all the papers were full of reviews

– and good ones at that. Perhaps if I quote from one or two this will be as good a way as any of conveying what 'Demelza's Baby' was all about: First from the *Daily Telegraph* by Sean Day-Lewis.

'It may have been coincidence that the idealised view of the homosexual companionship of Sir Angus Wilson and Tony Garrett in *The Other Half* last week should be followed last night by a *Forty Minutes* documentary giving a still more lyrical account of a lesbian partnership. Yet though the two films had different emphases they shared a calm acceptance refreshingly distant from the clamour of "gay rights" campaigning.

'Indeed "Demelza's Baby" (BBC 2) was an idyllic creation by Richard Lightbody in which the tender sympathy between Demelza and her friend Judy was signalled with a physical candour that made the pictures more expressive than the words. The background of Cornish coastline in benevolent summer greatly helped the mood.

'Past and future difficulties were not allowed to intrude. Judy's café in Penzance did not look to be a gold mine and I guess that Demelza earned even less as an enthusiastic player of the bongo drums in an Afro-Cornish rock group. Neither of the women in their interesting 30's seemed over confident about the long-term prospect of their love affair.

'For the duration of the film at least they were brought together by the baby of the title. "I was in a situation that was extraordinary and I got pregnant that night," said Demelza mysteriously. "The father feels he has helped two people out." And the infant Morgan could not have been better loved and cared for through his first six months.

'The censorious, noting his absence from the touching physical togetherness of the final seashore sequence, may see him as a suitable case for treatment some time in the future. But these were both demonstrably sensitive women, aware in advance of the impending pressures on their son. When one considers the resilience needed by the offspring of so many heterosexual marriages, Demelza's baby is not badly placed.'

Another thoughtful review by Maureen Paton appeared in the *Daily Express*, which ended:

'They clearly live just for each other and the baby, which turned out to be a handsome little boy. Their alternative life styles – Demelza's a rock drummer, Judy runs a wholefood café – obviously helps to keep the world at bay.

'But how most folk view the unorthodox family set up was never properly broached because the girls seemed too shy to contemplate it – content to stow away in their little gingerbread house and indulge in domestic bliss like any ordinary couple.

'Demelza called Judy the child's "second mother". Judy was more circumspect. "He feels he belongs to me – that's a much better way of putting it," she said with eminent good sense.

'Nice to see the baby's point of view getting priority for a change, when these two had every reason to get neurotic about their own roles.

' "I didn't emerge with the same sexuality as my parents so I suppose Morgan will go his own way," added Judy, presumably having learned tolerance the hard way.

'He's already a very happy baby and I found the tale a touching one. I hope life treats them kindly in the future, which is when the problems will really begin.'

Finally I'd like to quote part of the review in our local paper, the *Western Morning News*, by Allan Hermon:

'The documentary tackled a difficult subject forthrightly and with a measure of respect for the couple. This was partly due to the producer's obvious regard for the odd twosome and partly to the care taken by the film editor, Jane Val Baker, who is Demelza's sister. ...

'I hope the film unit will catch up with the couple in one or two years time so that we can see how they have coped with domestic problems. For Demelza at home with the baby while Judy goes out to work it won't be as easy as playing the African drums in the local band or dodging the waves on the seashore.'

And there it is, the rather public story of 'Demelza's Baby'. So far, I'm glad to report this unusual little family unit continues to flourish – and Morgan really is a beautiful baby!

IV

Cornwall for the Cornish

Cornish nationalism is on the move again, with many members of Mebyon Kernow winning seats at local elections. Although I am not a full scale nationalist I have always been drawn by the romantic side of such movements – though at the same time I can see some of the absurdities. Whether or not the Cornish nationalists will ever attain the power of their brothers and sisters in Wales and Scotland remains to be seen. I have my doubts because there is no longer a living Cornish language, despite valiant efforts by the Old Cornwall Societies.

When my interest in Cornish nationalism was first kindled, soon after I settled in the county, I happened to meet up with a BBC producer, John Gibson, and somehow we got talking on the subject. 'I tell you what,' he said to me, and was obviously in earnest, 'why don't you write us a play about it all?'

At first I pretended not to be interested, but of course I was – actually to be invited to write something is always a great temptation, and by the BBC, too. For several weeks, indeed months I went about thinking around the idea – then one day I sat at my desk and began work. The result was a radio play, *Cornwall for the Cornish*, which was broadcast by the BBC West Region and created quite a furore.

In the end I found that writing the play came quite easily – I simply sat at the typewriter and began with my narrator giving this spoof mock historical introduction (and went on from there):

The Cornish Rebellion of 1966, or the Cornish War of Independence as it is universally known in Cornwall, probably has its roots in the mysterious depths of Celtic mythology. However, for its more immediate sparking-point I think we should turn our attention to an evening in late September 1966. The time, about half-past eight on a Friday evening; the place, a hall at St Just, on the bleak, northern tip of the long Cornish peninsula. Here, where for centuries Cornishmen have burrowed into the bowels of the earth in their search for tin and copper – and where, most significantly, the influence of holiday-makers was very slight – several hundreds of loyal Cornish men and women were gathered to listen to a rather familiar voice ...

(*Sound of audience clapping, against which voice is heard*)

Freddie Grisewood

And now we'll have the next question, please, which comes from – ?

Trelawney

Trelawney, Thomas Trelawney.

Grisewood

Thomas Trelawney.

Trelawney

Cornwall was once a free country. For years it has suffered oppression at the hands of a Whitehall dictatorship. Would members of the team agree that it is high time Cornwall was given back its independence?

Grisewood

Cornwall was once a free country. For years it has suffered oppression at the hands of a Whitehall dictatorship. Would members of the team agree that it is high time Cornwall was given back its independence? ... Well, now, I'm sure our MPs will have something to say about this most interesting question. Er, Commander Higginbotham?

Higginbotham

Yes, of course, I believe very much in the freedom of the individual, and we in Whitehall must do all we can to cherish the individuality of each constituent part of our Great British heritage. But whether we should go as far as granting independence – well – I hardly think so.

Grisewood

What about you, John Robinson?

Robinson

You know, when my colleague, Commander Higginbotham, expresses those nice, easy, airy sentiments, I begin to understand how his party gets its votes – and it loses them! But let's face facts. We should have solidarity – we must all stand together, shoulder to shoulder. This is the age of the common man, and it doesn't matter whether he comes from Cornwall or Coventry.

Trelawney

What about answering the question?

Voices

Hear! Hear! (*First stirrings of obvious unrest*)

Robinson

I was just about to do so – as I was saying, it really is, surely, a bit archaic – well, shall I say, Ruritaniac – to speak of Cornwall for the – (*His words are drowned in a roar of disapproval*)

Grisewood

Well, perhaps we should consider a countryman's point of view. Er, come in Ralph Wightman.

Wightman

Well, there was Wessex, you know. I was coming down today through Devon and Cornwall, and looking out at the fields, and you know it struck me then, well, the soil of Devon may be a little redder than down here in Cornwall, but basically it's all country, isn't it, and we're all countrymen at heart, I fancy. But, you know, when I look at the question, you – know – I'm blessed – if – I quite know –

Voice

Course you don't! Just another furriner. Three cheers for Trelawney! Hip – hip *hooray*!

(*Voices join in the cheering. Above them Grisewood is heard vainly trying to continue*)

Grisewood

Now, please, St Just, you've been a wonderful audience up to now, so please don't spoil it. We thought you had come here to hear us, not *vice versa*. Now, the next question, which is ... ? er ... from ... ?

Trelawney

No you bloomin' well don't. It edn't right. I demand, in the name of Cornwall, that my question is fairly answered. (*Loud chorus of assent*)

Grisewood

Now, Trelawney, I beg of you, please ...

(*The noise rises up to a crescendo of shouts and cheers, noises and rumblings, voices swelling up into a great surge of song*)

Voices

And shall Trelawney die?
Ten thousand Cornishmen
Shall know the reason why!

(*The song ends to general pandemonium, startled cries of protest and help from speakers, noise of furniture being turned over, and programme is faded away)*

Narrator

The same night the rebels of St Just marched around Land's End peninsula gathering volunteers for what became known eventually as the A30 March. The ringleaders belonged to the Cornish Underground Movement. According to some of the more devout Cornish Nationalists, this has been in existence ever since the famous Western Rising of 1549. However, there is no doubt that guerillas were very active in the early part of 1966. How else is one to account for the fact that when the rebellion finally took place not a single British Army vehicle in Cornwall would start, while all the English guns kept in storage were found to be without any triggers? Not to mention petrol cans filled with water, tanks minus caterpillar tracks, aeroplanes with wings missing, and so forth. Over now to our recently rebuilt Truro Studio, where Tom Salmon is waiting for us to carry on our story.

Salmon

I have with me here in the studio tonight one of the leaders of the Cornish Underground Movement during the recent conflict. He is Mr Sampson Pengelly, of St Hilary, and well-known by now to the general public as the author of the best-selling adventure book, *I Nearly Sank the British Fleet at Plymouth*. Mr Pengelly, we all know your gallant story about the British Fleet episode. But there was, I believe, another of your exploits which you consider was even more remarkable, and for which you were, in fact, awarded the Grand Order of the Cornish Chough?

Pengelly

That's right. I destroyed two hundred and forty eight English motorists, all by meself.

Salmon

What was the actual method you used, Mr Pengelly?

Pengelly

Well, you know the big car park beside Penzance Harbour? Matter of fact, they filled in half the harbour to make the car park, you know. Well, it was simple, really. 'Twas August, height of the holiday season, place was thick with foreign cars. One evening, soon as it was dark, I re-arranged all the signs, you know, 'Exit', 'This Way Out', 'Turn Left' – and that sort of thing. Well, you know the English, they'm always doing what they'm told. So, one by one they got in their cars to drive off and went straight into the harbour. Lovely, it was – in they went, plop, plop, plop. Course, it was pretty deep, tide was in and all that, made things easier.

Salmon

Has this sort of thing been happening anywhere else in Cornwall, Mr Pengelly?

Pengelly

Oh, yes. The Roskelly gang, up to Looe, they used to put a tree across the branch line every evening, catch the trippers coming back on the half-past seven train from Liskeard. And Bob Pascoe, he was cook at a big hotel over to Falmouth, he used to wander around the beaches putting home-made time bombs under the visitors' deck chairs. Oh, we gave them a lively time, all right.

Salmon

Well, obviously you did, Mr Pengelly, and may I thank you very much for sparing us a few moments from your very valuable time.

Pengelly

Oh, that's all right, me old dear.

Narrator

If we look through the Cornish history books published during the period of secession, we can find many other stories similar to Mr Pengelly's – such as Miss Loveday Godolphin, Carnival Queen of Porthleven, whose own vital statistics were sufficiently impressive to extract rather more military statistics from several key members of the Royal Naval Station at Culdrose. In fact, individual enterprise was, as one might expect, the keynote of the Cornish Rebellion: but its swift success was largely due to one especially enterprising individual. I refer, of course, to Tom Gomery. Every Cornish schoolboy knows the romantic story of the bus conductor on the Penzance-Mousehole route, who rose from the depot (so to speak) to wield Cornwall's first, and last, field marshal's baton. Fortunately, we have preserved the voice of Field-Marshal Tommy, as he is affectionately known to millions, from his post-war speeches on the Cornish radio, as monitored by the BBC. The Field-Marshal was giving one of his typically modest accounts of 'My Victory March from Mousehole to the Banks of the Tamar'.

(*Sound of tuning in to programme, rather varied reception, then a slow, broad Cornish voice, reminiscent in style and delivery of a certain T.V. talks series, by a famous British commander.*)

Tom Gomery

It is now September 1966, and I felt, as captain of our team, the time had come to deliver one final, decisive knock-out blow. You see, I knew our softening-up process had thoroughly undermined our enemy's resistance; we had them really groggy. It was the end of the holiday season, so we need expect little opposition from the boarding-house keepers, about whose allegiance we were a little uncertain. Now, indeed, was the time to strike ...
(*Break for a moment back to Narrator*)

Narrator

After describing some of the preliminary skirmishes, like the sinking of all pleasure boats in the River Fal by units of the Mevagissey fishing fleet, and the padlocking of most of the main police forces inside their own stations, Field-Marshal Tommy continued:

(*Crackling sound and back to the Field-Marshal*)

Gomery

This was the moment I had been awaiting. I can remember now standing at the door of my caravan on Marazion Beach, looking at the dawn, and saying, in a voice sufficiently loud for my adjutant to make this note in his war diary: 'This is it, Bert' … I thereupon walked to the nearest telephone box, rang up Driver Lugg, at the Western National Bus Station, in Penzance, and the wheels were – literally – set in motion. Within an hour my army of double-decker buses were on the road – to be more precise, on the A30 road. My battle orders were brief, and, I like to think, to the point. 'Knock them for six across the Tamar.'

(*Crackling and back to Narrator*)

Narrator

The Field-Marshal was a man of his word, and by six o'clock on the evening of that fateful day in September 1966, his double-decker buses were in command of the whole of Cornwall and had blocked every road across the new national border – and, indeed, as everyone now knows, the next morning witnessed the signing of the Anglo-Cornish Peace Treaty at Launceston YMCA. But first let us consider for a moment what was happening on the other side of that fateful frontier. What, for instance, was going on in the nerve centre of the English democratic system, the House of Commons?

Reader

The honourable Member for Ambridge continued: 'Will the Minister kindly inform the House why flower pots sold as butter dishes are still exempt from purchase tax?'

'If my Right Honourable Friend had paid attention to my speech last Friday he would know that under sub-section eight of para – ' At this point the honourable Member for Dimstock interrupted: 'Mr Speaker, I beg leave to interrupt the business of the House to consider the grave situation that has arisen in the West Country.' There were cries of: 'Order, order,' and after the Speaker had regained control, he said: 'I am afraid I must rule that interruption out of order. Kindly proceed with the business of the House.'

'Under sub-section eight of paragraph nine, clause sixteen, of the Purchase Tax Exemption Bill, whereas it is an offence to market as a butter-dish an article which is patently not a butter-dish, there is another clause in the same Bill which provides that if a flower pot be used for some other purpose then it is not necessarily subject to tax.'

(*End of reading from Hansard*)

Narrator

As these very words were being spoken in Westminster, Cornish irregulars had occupied Culdrose and St Mawgan Airports. Frogmen had blown up the Torpoint Ferry and a group of quarry workers had blown up several yards of main line railway track. Nevertheless, the English Government were keeping abreast of world affairs, as this recorded interview with the Foreign Minister at London Airport may show.

(*Sound of humming and scuffling and bustle and jet engines*)

Interviewer

Now, sir, I wonder if you might give our listeners a very brief resumé of your itinerary. You're going first to Paris, I understand.

Foreign Minister

Yes, that's right. I'm going to Paris to have talks with my opposite number there, and then I shall be flying on to Bonn and after that Vienna, and after that to Moscow, where I expect to have conversations with the Soviet leaders, and after that I shall be flying to India and Burma, and later on I hope to call in on Australia and perhaps New Zealand before making this special visit to Washington.

Interviewer

Well, sir, that sounds a pretty full schedule. I suppose that means you won't personally be able to deal with the trouble in Cornwall?

Foreign Minister

Trouble in Cornwall? Oh, yes, of course – trouble in Cornwall. Well, that would be a matter for the Home Office.

Interviewer

And what, sir, do you hope to achieve by your journey?

Foreign Minister

I want to sound out my opposite numbers, to see what they are thinking.

Interviewer

About anything in particular?

Foreign Minister

No – I can't really say at this stage, you understand.

Interviewer

Of course. Thank you, sir. (*Fade*)

Narrator

That evening the Home Secretary stated at a Press Conference that since the River Tamar had now assumed the status of an international frontier, the Cornish incident was now a matter for the Foreign Office.

Narrator

In due course, as the world well knows, by appealing to the United Nations, Cornwall established herself in such a morally impregnable position that it became virtually impossible for the English Government to take such action as bombardment or re-invasion. The frontier to Cornwall was immediately closed and it was at once made clear that no visas would be issued to any English people who wished to visit the new state – a ban on holiday-makers that was to be the first shot fired in the economic counter-offensive. However, for the moment the Cornish were far too elated to worry about matters of that sort. Members of Old Cornwall Societies lit bonfires on every conceivable hilltop. There was guise-dancing in the streets of St Ives, the Hobby Horse was brought out specially for the occasion at Padstow, the Helston folk did the Furry Dance all through the night. In honour of victory, the pubs opened all hours, local bakers made free Cornish pasties for all, and schoolchildren were given a week's holiday ... The BBC's Redruth transmitter had been stormed by the first bus-load of irregulars who passed that way. The Engineer-in-Charge gallantly locked the doors, but could not resist the overwhelming forces of New Cornwall. He has since been decorated with the Reith Medal for steadfastness. Once in Cornish hands, rebel transmissions began with a live outside broadcast from Penzance.
(*Sound of wild cheering and shouting and singing, fireworks let off, hooters, etc., commentator's voice in broad Cornish*)

Bernard Fishwick

I'm speaking to you from the balcony of St John's Hall. My word, you never seen such a sight, me dears; there's a proper feast – proper job.
(*Sound of cheering, singing, etc.*)

Fishwick

Hullo, hullo, what's this – yes, I can just see – they're bringing

along some more prisoners. Yes, there they are, I can see them now, marching along in treble file – very surprisin', really, how many non-Cornish people have managed to get into Cornwall, even this end. We've just had one column go by, and I counted four hundred in that, and now this one's just as long. Now, wait a minute. I'll see if there be anyone I know – oh, yes, yes, there's two of the local bank managers, oh, and there's the president of the local chamber of trade, and Mr Brown, manager of the gasworks, and the chairman of the electricity board – my word, we're going to see some new faces behind the local bars, too, judging by the number of publicans in the procession. Still, it's Cornwall for the Cornish now, and we can't afford to be sentimental – ah, there goes the former MP; I expect they'll hang 'ee. But most of them, I understand, are marching down to the harbour to be taken aboard the *Scillonian* and shipped to one of the more remote of the Isles of Scilly. Well, I don't think they're doing too badly; lovely climate on the Scillies – just think, they might have been sent back to London smog.
(*Sound of massed voices*)

(*Singing fades away*)

Narrator

Yes, indeed, Cornwall is not likely to forget its own Victory Day. However, the next morning a rather more sober assessment of the situation was necessary. One of the founders of the Cornish Free State Republic, Mr Jim Pender, was recently interviewed in the television programme *Tonight*.

Derek Hart

Mr Pender, I understand you were actually present at the historic first meeting of the Cornish Free State Republic Government?

Pender

Yes. 'Twas held on a boat in Falmouth Harbour.

Derek Hart

On a boat? Surely that's a rather unusual place for a Government to meet? I mean, was no attempt made to meet ashore?

Pender

Oh, aye. But mind you, no one could agree on anywhere else. It edn't fair, they'd say, it edn't fair. Fellows from Truro, they wants it in Truro, 'course – and the fellows from Camborne, nacherally they wants it at Camborne – and them from Penzance, they wants it there – oh, 'twas a right carry on, I well remembers.

Derek Hart

Well, you have told us where the others wanted it held, but where did *you* think it should be held, Mr Pender?

Pender

Oh, Newlyn, of course. I'm a Newlyn man, see.

Derek Hart

Well, now look, when your Government met on this boat in Falmouth Harbour, what was the first business that you discussed?

Pender

Let's see, now, well, 'course, the first business we did talk about was where we should make the Government headquarters. We went at it 'ammer an' tongs, we did, from ten in the morning till nearly seven o'clock at night, afore we finally decided on a place.

Derek Hart

And that was where?

Pender

A boat in Falmouth harbour.

Derek Hart

Was that the same boat?

Pender

Yes.

Derek Hart

Well, Mr Pender, you presumably found this meeting pretty exciting, didn't you? Were all the leaders there?

Pender

Let's see. Yes, quite a lot o' folk. Bill Wearne, from Sennen; and Tom Laity, from Lamorna; and Percy Hitchens, from up Paul Hill. Then, of course, there were quite a few furriners.

Derek Hart

Where did these foreigners come from?

Pender

You know, fellers from up country, Camborne and Redruth way, Bodmin – even outlandish places like Tintagel and Bude. Pretty odd lot, I thought. Niver did like foreigners, not me. Likes my own kind, I do, you know, Newlyn folk. One Newlyn feller, 'ee do be worth a handful o' up-country skate.

Derek Hart

I see. Well, Mr Pender, we must thank you very much indeed.

Narrator

Looking back at newspaper reports of those early days, it appears that Mr Pender's picture was an accurate one. At one stage there were so many interests insisting on being represented in the Government, that on several occasions there was a serious danger of the Cornish Free State Republic sinking without trace in the River Fal. Later, these numbers were drastically pruned, for safety's sake, but there remained many conflicting interests at work, notably in the financial field. Of course, this is a very specialised field, so not long ago we sent our industrial correspondent, Kenneth Hudson, to interview Mr Joseph Pentavish, of Truro.

Hudson

Mr Pentavish, I believe you held the unique honour of having been Treasurer to the Cornwall County Council before the Rebellion; Treasurer to the Cornish Free State Republic during the period of the government, and now once again Treasurer to the present Cornwall County Council. Now I know that your name was originally MacTavish, but you changed it to Pentavish when you became a naturalised Cornishman, but I see you still retain your very definite native accent. Now tell me, Mr Pentavish, how is it that you, a Scotsman, held such a position in Cornish government?

Pentavish

Och, I wasna the only Scotsman to stay in Cornwall, ye know. There was a referendum held, ye see, and those who didna want to leave, were allowed to stay if they became naturalised citizens. Mind ye, I was pretty indispensable, anyway, and, well, they knew that at the County Hall.

Hudson

Yes, Mr Pentavish, that may well be, but, surely, with the change to independence, there must have been some big economic changes?

Pentavish

Och, I dinna think so. Not really. You see, we nationalised the china clay pits. The same with tin – and, as ye know, there's a big demand for Cornish tin in the world markets – In the same way that American men drink Scotch whisky and American women wear tartan trousers. It's the sentimental value, you see.

Hudson

So really you don't feel that Cornwall was very much worse off as a free country than as an English county?

Pentavish

Not a bit of it. No not really, except for one thing. We did miss the business with English holiday-makers, when they were forbidden to come to Cornwall. Mind you, we still got a lot of folk from overseas, but I must admit it wasn't just the same thing. Still, we survived a'right.

Narrator

Seen in a sober historical perspective, this view has been generally accepted. Where dissensions occurred, in those early days, was in spheres rather outside the economic one. Here, for instance, is part of a series of interesting, uncensored discussions broadcast by the Cornish Broadcasting Corporation in the carefree early days of the revolution.

Chairman

I'm now going to ask some typical members of our younger generation to sum up their views on the moulding of our new republic. Er, Major-General Andrewartha?

Andrewartha

Well, first, of course, I think we must exterminate all traces of the English. It's no use their changing their names to Pen-Smith and Tre-Brown, and all that; we must root them out and destroy them without mercy. Then I'd introduce conscription to build up an army to liberate the oppressed peoples of Wales. After that, Brittany.

Chairman

Thank you for the military point of view, Major-General Andrewartha. Now, what about the educational programme? Mr Treveska, what do you think?

Treveska

First, I propose we drop all English subjects from the curriculum. Every Cornish child should be taught its own native language; that seems logical enough. Then, of course, you'd need a Cornish University, Cornish-speaking, of course. Yes.

Chairman

Thank you, Mr Treveska. Now to the artistic side of life. Mr Sampson, as Curator of Cornwall's First National Art Gallery, how far has New Cornwall progressed in this direction?

Sampson

Our first step, of course, has been the ruthless elimination of all non-Cornish artists. Some, as you know, offered resistance and had to be executed; the remainder we've treated very leniently – we've corralled them all in the middle of Bodmin Moor and left them to paint to their heart's content. Mind you, for the moment this *has* posed some problems, as both members of our New Cornish Art Movement are over eighty. However, I have my eye on several promising youngsters.

Chairman

And, finally, to the very important field of literature. Mr T. Davies Roskelly, as editor of the new *avant garde* Cornish literary monthly, *Mebyon Kernow*, what do you feel of the possibilities of a Cornish literary renaissance?

Roskelly

Very hopeful, very hopeful. At first we suffered the grave disadvantage that most of our literary native sons chose to write about Cornwall and live elsewhere. Similarly, the small number of foreign English writers resident here soon departed when independence brought with it a slight fall in the standard of living. But privation makes one look at oneself for what one really is, and I cannot help but feel the long-term effects will be most salutory.

Narrator

In those early days a study of the programmes of the New Cornish Broadcasting Corporation gives a fascinating picture of the birth-pangs of an embryo state. Obviously the leaders realised that their followers would have to be gently weaned on to their new cultural diet; at least this would appear to be the explanation for a number of programmes, such as *Mrs Hosking's Diary*, in which a Cornish doctor's wife records the daily happenings in the life of her family; *The Blewetts*, a story of country folk; and some of the lighter programmes, like *Scilly Island Discs*, *Educating Loveday* and *Life with the Trevorrow's*. On the other hand, real enterprise was shown in the presentation of documentary programmes, such as 'Shakespeare was a Cornishman' and 'Justice for Richard Trevithick'. Later on, of course, it became progressively more difficult to follow the *Cornish Radio Times* ... like *The Cornishman* and *West Briton* newspapers fell into the hands of members of the Pure Cornish for Pure Cornish Society, who started bringing out editions printed entirely in Cornish. For a time, indeed, they even dictated the affairs of the broadcasting service itself. These and similar developments caused so much confusion that the new Government decided to make the introduction of Cornish a long-term measure. Nevertheless, the idealogical party line was very firmly enforced. Who was not for Cornwall was against Cornwall, as Mr Matthew Lugg, a Newlyn fisherman, testified in a broadcast from our Plymouth studios, after he had swum to freedom.

Interviewer

Mr Lugg, what made you decide to leave your native land?

Lugg

Well, mister, I never 'ad much choice. I wuz sittin' with me mate, Sam Richards, 'avin' a quiet drink one night, an' I ken remember jess wot Sam were sayin' – an' then we 'ear them comin'.

Interviewer

Who did you hear coming?

Lugg

Why, them storm-troopers, course. They be all over the place in Cornwall, you know; if you get be'ind with yer rates or yer tax, or if you do anythin' a bit wrong like, they'll be outside of yer door afore you can say Cornwall for ever. I ken see Sam now. Coo, he was sitting there, a picture o' injured innocence, an four o' them big 'usky fellers, they just picked 'im up like a feather an' took 'im off.

Interviewer

What happened to him?

Lugg

Well, nobody knows really – but they do say he was throwed in off the quay. An' that were the end o' poor Sam ... Next day I thinks to meself, time I went – an' 'ere I be.

Narrator

The Cornish were undoubtedly rather touchy about their national status at first, but they really had no need to worry. Within a month of the famous A30 Drive, Cornwall's ambassadors were firmly installed at Moscow, Peking, Washington, Rome, Paris and other world capitals, together with their cultural attachés. In the face of such universal acceptance, the British, always realistic in such matters, proposed opening trade negotiations, although they still kept up their embargo on holiday-makers. Otherwise, however,

Cornwall's national planners could feel well pleased with developments. Exports were up, the fishing fleets were almost doubled, and prospects generally were bright. Cornwall for the Cornish was a theme applied in every possible sphere. On the home front, too, the authorities were anxious to encourage all cultural activities, and valiant work was done to this end by the current Grand Bard of the Cornish Gorsedd. Here is a CBC recording of one of the crownings.

(*Sound of crowds cheering, then fades*)

Grand Bard

Kernow, Cres, ha Kerensa – which, in case there are still some of you lacking in a full knowledge of your native language, I may translate as: 'Cornwall, Peace and Friendship'. Tonight we are gathered at Perran Round to witness yet another crowning of the bards for their outstanding cultural services to their native land. Now, if you will kindly step forward, please: Thomas Howard Eddy, I crown you Bard of the Cornish Pasty. Wilhelmina Georgina Pearce, I crown you Bard of the Flute. Samuel Pascoe Pascoe, I crown you Bard of the Postal Services. Maria Rosalie Trezise, I crown you Bard of the Knitting Needle. (*As his voice drones on it is faded away*)

Narrator

This was the time of a great literary and artistic renaissance. No one who reads them will ever forget the romantic poems of Clementine O'Milley Tregenza, the fisherman's daughter-poet of Sennen Cove; or the lurid melodramatic Cornish novels of Matthew Penna, the drapery assistant, from St Austell; or the twelve-volume *History of the Cornish-Speaking Peoples*, by Winston Chapelhill. Unfortunately, we haven't time to read any of their work tonight, but some idea of the intense interest in artistic affairs may be gained from this recording of an interview in the seven o'clock Cornish Newsreel.

Interviewer

Today I have made the precarious journey across the wild Zennor moors to the lonely carn which may one day become a Cornish shrine. For here, where the winds howl bleakly across the boulder-strewn hill tops, and there is a view of the distant Atlantic ocean, when the mist rises, here, tucked quite snugly, I must say, into this very old carn – here is the home of Cornwall's greatest living primitive painter, Tom Toms, Mr Toms, how long have you lived up here?

Toms

Well, ever since I was turned out o' me council 'ouse by the West Penwith Council for getting behind with me rent.

Interviewer

Yes, yes, what I really meant, Mr Toms, was – when did you feel the – the call to take up your great work?

Toms

Well, as I say, when I was turned out of me house by the West Penwith Council ...

Interviewer (Hastily)

Well, Mr Toms, I see you are drying some of your paintings in the mid-day sunshine. What a charming picture. Of course, these are all painted on bed sheets, I know. Most interesting. Mr Toms, I feel sure our listeners would be very interested to know about your methods of painting your, er, very primitive pictures. Now, exactly how do you go about it?

Toms

Well, I hangs up the sheet like this, see, and then I picks up a brush and I dips it in the paint and then I flicks it on the sheet like this, you see? Easy, really. Why, if I 'ad enough sheets I could do thousands – *thousands* a day I could do.

Interviewer

Really, Mr Toms. Thousands?

Toms

Yes, thousands. Course, that's the trouble – supplies. I mean bed sheets cost money you know. Any old sheets? I do say. They people's very good sometimes, they do give me some. Mind you, some of them smell something awful. I got to go and wash them in the sea.

Interviewer

What, you mean before painting your inimitable pictures you *wash* them in the green sea water? I suppose you feel that impregnates them with some kind of mysterious Cornish quality, something of that eerie mysticism which the poet has in mind, perhaps, in those lines – how do they go …

Toms

I dunno about that. Takes away the smell, that's what I says. (*Fade away*)

Narrator

The development of a new national culture was, of course, a complex matter, and in some spheres there were … difficulties. For instance, well-meant, but ill-judged, attempts to encourage regional pride resulted in this sort of thing, as revealed in this Rugby commentary by Alan Gibson:

Gibson

My word, that was a near miss. Pengelly went down like a stone. The ambulance men are taking him off the field now. That makes the seventeenth casualty this afternoon. Well, ladies and gentlemen, this semi-final All-Cornwall Rugby Cup Tie between Redruth and Penzance-Newlyn Pirates is a real ding-dong affair. Ah, I see the referee has called for more police reinforcements. Now there is a solid ring of policemen right round the pitch. It must be a little difficult for some of the spectators to see play. But then, of course, as we all know, previous experience in this great national contest has shown the need for preserving public order. After the lynching of three players at the match between Falmouth and Penryn, and the stabbings at Truro and Newquay, the authorities decided to take serious action. That, of course, explains why there are machine-gun posts set up at each corner of the field, ready to open fire, if necessary. (*Sudden outbreak of cheering from crowd*)

Now here's some excitement. Stevens, the Pirates' wing-half, has got the ball. He's racing away, he's beaten one man, and another … (*Crowd's cheers grow more excited*)

He's away! He's clean away down the wing. I don't think they're going to be able to catch him – (*Suddenly there is a great Ooooooh! from the crowd*)

Oh, dear – well, ladies and gentlemen, that was most dramatic. Stevens was clean away then and undoubtedly would have scored the winning try when one of the Redruth players pulled out a lasso and lassoed Stevens from thirty feet – I must say it was a pretty piece of ropework. Of course, lassoing a player on the run is even against the Cornish Rugby rules, and the referee has quite rightly given a foul. But I very much fear that Redruth have lost their golden opportunity.

(*Sound of muttering and restiveness among the crowd*)

Yes, I'm rather afraid that tempers are mounting. There's only seconds left – ah, there's the whistle. (*Shrill sound of whistle being blown, followed by outbreak of jeers and catcalls, rising to pandemonium*)

I fear the crowd look like getting out of hand. I just saw three of the Penzance players being set upon – my word, things are getting really out of hand – I can see several casualties – oh, and there's the referee lying unconscious on the pitch – now the crowd are rushing towards the grandstand. I'm very much afraid, yes, I can see the local commander giving the signal to fire. I very much fear – (*His words are drowned by the staccato sound of machine gun fire sweeping the crowd. Sound fades away*)

Narrator

Shootings, lynchings, stabbings – there seemed no limit to the display of partisanship at these various regional events. Before long the Cornish Government was forced to ban all sports meetings, and, indeed, competitive events of any kind. Possibly they under-estimated the strength of this inter-regional competitive spirit. Now, however, there developed a series of widening breaches between the various Cornish localities. This was reflected in many ways. For instance foreign newspapers were rather startled to receive advertisements reading something like this:

Voice

Come to sunny St Ives! Enjoy sunshine and freedom away from the dirt and squalor of inland Cornwall, with its derelict mines and uneducated natives.

Second Voice

Explore mysterious Redruth, home of all that's best in ancient Cornwall – and far from the sordid sophistication of St Ives and its ogling artists.

Third Voice

Trip the light fantastic – at Helston Flora Day! Cornwall's gayest, maddest round – come, dance the hours away. From dawn to midnight. Overseas visitors welcomed.

Narrator

Soon this element of competition extended far beyond newspaper advertisements. It wasn't long before the respective fishing fleets were going off on their trips quite heavily armed with machine guns and cannons – which they did not hesitate to use if they came across their rivals. In this way the fleets began to decline in numbers. In the same way, Cornwall's half-a-dozen newspapers began taking extremely hostile attitudes to one another; while the Cornish radio programmes were constantly being interrupted by pirate stations, shouting out such slogans as: 'Penzance for Ever!' or 'Truro Cathedral Must Go!' or 'Mevagissey Stinks!' The effect of all this on the Cornish Government's ambitious plans for attracting overseas holiday-makers was unfortunate.

News Announcer

This is the Cornish Broadcasting Corporation. Good evening. Here is the seven o'clock news for today, Tuesday, July 2nd. Sunny weather is reported from all the leading Cornish holiday resorts. At Penzance the Town Clerk welcomed a large party of visitors from America, and expressed the hope they would have an enjoyable stay, despite the loss of several of their members, shot by snipers along the Eastern Green Approach. He assured the visitors that members of the Penzance Citizens' Armed Brigades would provide them with a full escort wherever they went, in case of attacks of marauding bands from Newlyn and Mousehole. He denied rumours that the town's water supply had been poisoned by saboteurs from St Ives, and gave a categorical assurance that the extensive bomb damage to Market Jew Street would be cleared in time for the carnival procession ... At Falmouth today the Mayor strongly denied stories that six Falmouth pleasure boats had been attacked and sunk travelling up the River Fal to Truro. One boat had actually been sunk, said the Mayor, and most of the occupants had been saved. In any case, the Falmouth Corporation, under its Emergency Measures now in force, was arranging for all future pleasure trips to have a strong escort of armed motor cruisers. This was the reason, he added, why all private shipping in the area had been commandeered, as it was the Corporation's intention, in the Mayor's words, to provide the town with a Falmouth Navy, in the fullest traditions of the town's distinguished maritime history ... At St Austell, where road blocks have been set up around the town and passports issued to all residents, our correspondent reports all quiet, but at Looe, desultory fighting between the East and West banks continues. Soon it became dangerous to travel from one town to another. The Cornish Government became thoroughly alarmed ... and this may be the reason for their decision to proceed with the trial for high treason of Mrs Lily Menhenitt. Under Cornish regulations, proceedings of such trials were allowed to be broadcast, so we can actually listen now to the Cornish Attorney-General's cross-examination of Mrs Menhenitt:

(*Sound of coughing in background, humming and hawing, then a hush as cross-examination develops*)

Attorney-General

Mrs Menhenitt, you are the chairman of a somewhat nebulous body, calling itself, I believe, the League of Landladies, Landlords and Bed and Breakfast Providers?

Mrs Menhenitt

I'm sure I doan't know ef it's neb – whatever et be – but et edn't anything for 'ee to laugh at, mister, 'cos we do 'ave thousands of members iverywhere, that we do – aye, in every town and village in Cornwall.

Attorney-General

Ahem, yes, quite. Mrs Menhenitt, you are here to answer questions, not to make propoganda.

Mrs Menhenitt

Someone's got to make propoganda. The rate you folk be going on there'll be –

Judge

Silence, prisoner! You must answer the questions.

Attorney-General

Now, Mrs Menhenitt, I want to take you back to a certain afternoon in Newquay, in the Beach Cafe, when, it is our allegation, you were heard to make subversive remarks to a group of other ladies.

Mrs Menhenitt (Spiritedly)

If you mean Mrs Rowe and Miss Trembath, why we wus discussin' all these terrible cancellations we bin 'aving. Oh, my dear life, says Mrs Rowe, I bin an 'ad another family cryin' off today, that makes the fourth we 'ad this week. An' Miss Trembath, she says: 'Yes, 'tis the first time for ten years we niver had no August booking at all,' and I says –

Attorney-General

Mrs Menhenitt, if you will allow me, as the prosecutor, to conduct these proceedings, I was about to quote the words that you are alleged to have said. They were – and I want you to listen very carefully, for I hope you realise that in this trial your very life is in danger – the words were: 'Time we landladies got together, united we stand, divided we fall.' Now, Mrs Menhenitt, I ask you to think carefully – did you or did you not make that most treasonable remark?

Mrs Menhenitt

'Course I did, an ef et 'edn't time someone got together to save us from oursells, then I doan't know wot else ... Why, mister, do 'ee know this be the worst holiday season we iver 'ad? 'Ow do 'ee think we landladies be going to keep agoing?

Voices

Hear! Hear!

Judge

Silence in court!

Attorney-General

Mrs Menhenitt, I ask you to consider the gravity of your position.

Mrs Menhenitt

What about the gravity of *all* our positions? S'posin' I doan't get no visitors this season – 'ow do you 'spect me to feed me family? Pay me rates? Pay me electricity? Now, then, mister, you tell me that.

Voices

That's right – three cheers for Mrs Menhenitt! Long live the League of Landladies!

Judge

This is monstrous. Unless these interruptions cease at once, I will have to clear the court…

Narrator

Well, the interruptions did not desist. The judge did clear the court, and Mrs Menhenitt was – again, I would suggest, most unwisely – sentenced to death. Of course, the Cornish Government quickly realised it had gone too far from the volume of protests, but by then it was too late. Mrs Menhenitt provided just that element of martyrdom needed to stir up all those quixotic feelings that lurk in every Cornish heart. Forgotten were all the intertown rivalries, the blood feuds, and so on – here was something to unite all Cornish men and Cornish women solidly against their own divided Government. Moreover, the League of Landladies, Landlords and Bed and Breakfast Providers cut clear across all classes and creeds – it was, indeed, as everyone realised, the most truly representative body in all Cornwall. As such, it soon felt itself powerful enough to open secret negotiations with the British Government. In return for a firm promise that all restrictions would be removed on British holidaymakers coming to Cornwall, the League promised full support for a British re-occupation of Cornwall.

When, in due course, cunningly choosing a Thursday afternoon, the general closing day in Cornwall, the British dropped several brigades of parachutists at strategic points, the opposition was negligible. Torn by internal dissensions, without the services of so many stalwarts killed or maimed on the Rugby fields, uncertain of how many units of the Cornish Navy could be spared from regular smuggling runs to the Continent, the Cornish could do nothing but give in gracefully. In June 1967, not too late for a bumper holiday season to be organised, Cornwall became once again England's first and last county, depending on the way you look at things. On the Saturday the English Prime Minister caught the Devon Riviera Express from Paddington and proceeded to Plymouth for the surrender ceremony. This was performed in the centre of the Tamar Road Bridge, now re-opened for traffic after so many months' idleness. It was a moving scene ...

Commentator

The Prime Minister has just stepped from his car. Behind are the two shining black coaches, the first containing his staff of Home Office advisers, the second those from the Foreign Office. And on the other side ... yes ... I can just see the Cornish Delegation alighting from their transport – oh! a double-decker bus – a curious choice. Still, the two parties are now approaching each other, towards the table set in the very centre of this magnificent bridge. I can just see the shiny white paper of the instrument of surrender itself, which, at any moment now, will receive the all important signature ... (*Fade*)

Narrator

The ceremony was completed with that sense of pageantry and occasion which has made Britain the Mecca for the tourists of the world. The English Government advisers, drawn up in two opposing ranks, with bowler hats impeccably straight and umbrellas at the furl. The Cornish delegation were no less impressive, although their turn-out expressed more their rugged individualism and the recent trading restrictions.

That night the whole re-united kingdom sat down in front of

their television sets and radio loudspeakers to await the Prime Minister.

Prime Minister

My friends, indeed, I may say my friends on both sides of the Tamar. This is for me a happy occasion, although, if I may be permitted a paradox – one that I sincerely wish the fates had never sought to make necessary. In the recent and painful past we both erred from the golden way of understanding and mutual respect. But now – and I trust for many years to come – we again face our destinies, hand in hand, ready to step forward in the direction of our shining future.

My Government and I have agreed that as a token of our new-found faith and fellowship, the body of Mrs Lily Menhenitt will be buried in Westminster Abbey, with all due pomp and ceremony, next to those whose glory has made the name of Britain ring out down the centuries.

Narrator

And so the tide of returning tourists beat upon moor and shore, until the roadsides proclaimed once again the good news: 'No vacancies' … Soon the rough grass and purple valerian healed the scars of battle and the last derelict double-decker found its way to the scrap-heap. The war was now a story across the saloon bar, a moral from the non-conformist pulpits and a gold-mine for the makers of Cornish mementoes …

V

Secret Worlds

All through our family life a daily event of the greatest importance has been the arrival of the postman – sometimes under rather unusual circumstances, as at the Old Sawmills near Fowey where the poor man had to walk a mile along a riverbank to reach our home. Here at the Mill House the postman has no walking to do at all, through the always open gates and up past the spinning water wheel to our front porch. There, invariably, he delivers a substantial batch of letters, usually held together by an elastic band, and then departs with a cheerful wave.

In the past the bulk of the letters were for myself – letters from publishers, from magazine editors, from fellow authors, from readers of my books, perhaps one or two welcome cheques – which was one reason why usually I rushed out to greet the postman. More recently, alas, with my continued illness, I have been unable to keep up my previous level of work, with the result that as my outgoings have decreased, so my incoming mail has also been considerably reduced. Now the letters that come are for the Misses Val Bakers of various initials, for Stephen and Gina, or for Alan or Gill – even for Jess, who gets an endless flow of catalogues from garden seed merchants. Myself I am lucky to get an odd editorial communication – even luckier still to get a cheque, other than my periodical payments from kind Peter Kimber, without whose sympathetic support I would be a lost cause indeed.

Fortunately, as the business correspondence has dried up, personal mail has somewhat increased as old friends, hearing of my problems, write to cheer me up in my doldrums. It is always heartening to get such missives especially from distant friends seldom seen, like Ken Moss up at Liverpool, or Donald Swan far away on his Scottish island of Cumbrae where with his wife Elizabeth he runs a pottery and paints pictures. As one gets older, indeed, the realisation comes that in the long run it is people who matter rather than business affairs.

Recently there arrived in my post a square-shaped blue envelope which was obviously a personal missive of some kind. Looking at the round rather flourishing writing I had a vague feeling of familiarity but could not place it. At last after guessing away I lost patience and opened the letter – and found it was a long awaited reply to a letter of mine which I must have sent at least three years back. It came from a long lost cousin of mine – Tom Eames Hughes, son of my favourite Uncle Harry, from Llanfairfechan, North Wales.

Tom had long since retired from the Civil Service (he had spent a lifetime working in various British embassies out in the Far East) and indeed must now, I reckoned, be practically in his eighties. This made it all the more pleasant to hear from him and to have brief news of his wife and family, and of some of my other scattered cousins.

Tom's long letter did more than interest and please me – it triggered off all sorts of old memories and reminded me of a rather fascinating aspect of my life – namely that over a period of sixty years in my typically Scorpionic ritualistic way, I have inhabited quite a series of separate and self-contained worlds – and that one of the most important of these had been my Llanfairfechan world.

For me this period will always be associated with my late teens. It was a time when I was in the fifth or sixth form at grammar school and had not yet begun my escapism, and this I certainly found up on the (for me) golden shores of North Wales. For several years, while I went on living my normal life down in London a part of me was always dreaming about Wales, and the inevitable long summer holiday I would hopefully spend up there (really long when I was still at school, rather curtailed alas when later on newspaper work confined my holiday to three weeks).

Looking back and remembering my own position as the only son of two rather separate parents I can see now that much of the attraction of Llanfairfechan was that in and around the place lived several cousins and uncles and aunts, so providing me with a much needed sense of 'family'. I loved my elderly Uncle Harry and Aunty Lil (my mother's older sister) and they always made me cheerfully welcome at their comfortable home in Park Crescent, hardly more than a stone's throw from Llanfairfechan beach and promenade. There was Tom and his younger sister Gladwyn, my two cousins – plus a bevy of other cousins living over at Conway, Peggy and Elizabeth and Basil. The latter became my special crony and the two of us took to camping out along the Cob (with frequent trips to Cynlas to enjoy some of Aunty Lil's hot *bara brief* bread or Welsh cake).

It is with Basil I associate some of my most beloved memories of those golden Llanfairfechan days. He and I were fond of going for scrambles up the beautiful Aber Falls, and sometimes further afield – once we gathered together a whole crowd of young friends and executed a midnight march over Bryn Mawr and several other mountains, stopping somewhere on the top to light a bonfire and cook sausages which we had brought with us – ending up by trooping down into Conway where Basil's parents, my Uncle Ivor and Aunty Marion, provided us all with a vast Welsh breakfast in their big house near the castle. With Basil, too, I began the habit every Saturday night of going over to Llandudno to enjoy the delights of an evening in Payne's Ballroom, preferably in the company of some attractive young lady (whom later with luck I could take for a romantic walk up the Great Orme, the headland protruding over the town).

Tennis was another of our preoccupations, the big event of the week being the weekly tournament on the Llanfairfechan public courts on the promenade. What titanic confrontations there were, too. My cousin Tom was almost up to professional standard and he usually won the tournaments. Once, playing with sexy Megan Davies, I got to the final and actually won – usually, though, I was like so many Britishers, a gallant loser.

Repeating these summer gatherings year after year we naturally accumulated quite a regular group of friends. Every morning we would foregather in a little cafe on a corner of the promenade to plan some daily outing. It was in that cafe, I remember, that the idea was born of broadening our summertime connections into an all the year round contact by forming an association, starting up our own news letter and so forth. Inevitably, because of my profession, I was made editor of the news letter, and so now I had an added pleasure over the long winter months of writing round all over the place gathering news of our various members' activities. I wish I had kept some copies of those dear old news letters!

Viewed in perspective I suppose I would have to admit that Llanfairfechan is quite an ordinary little seaside town, but for me in those years it became a magical place. There was even, shades of the past, a pierrot show on the pavilion – every year I fell in love with the *soubrette* as the leading lady was known. I fell in love rather easily those days and have a vague memory of a host of lovely Welsh girls, like Megan – Betti and Davida and, above all, Dwyfyrdd. The latter was the daughter of a Welsh vicar and quite the love of my life. Alas it was to be ever an unrequited love, and after many romantic wanderings up on the mountain tops (where I once bound our troth with a grass ring) we began to lose touch – since then I have not heard a word. Where are you, oh, where, darling Dwyfyrdd?

I suppose my Welsh world lasted four or five years before circumstances drew me away. Those circumstances provided the ingredient for another of my self-contained worlds – namely the world of newspapers. By now I had begun work as a junior reporter on the *Derby Evening Telegraph*, one of the Northcliffe string of provincial newspapers. From the moment, rather nervously, I entered the *Telegraph*'s massive building in the centre of Derby it was indeed like entering a completely self-contained world. The reporters' room, I soon found, was not only a madhouse, a bedlam of rattling typewriters and jangling 'phone bells – it was also a very, very exclusive club, to which I was now greatly honoured by being given membership. Of course as the new junior I got all the rotten jobs. The news editor, an alcoholic misery of a man, had a huge diary of each day's events in which he would pencil the initials of a reporter opposite whatever events he had to cover. My dream was to cover the exciting police courts – the reality was I had to report on funerals and weddings, both of which, if attended *ad infinitum*, lost all power to surprise or even move.

Usually I used to get a lift with the undertaker out to the funerals (where my job was to take a list of the mourners) and this enabled me to learn quite a lot of lively gossip of the trade – while at weddings, if I was lucky, I might get a welcome glass of champagne. But it was all hardly vintage journalism.

Gradually, thank goodness, my journalistic scope was allowed to widen. I began interviewing visiting celebrities like John McCormack the singer, or Amy Johnson the flyer – I covered political rallies and religious meetings – I even eventually became the paper's theatre critic. Because my shorthand was rather suspect I never really got on to the police court circuit, but otherwise I was soon 'blooded' in all directions.

Two of my favourite memories are of comparative disasters. Once I had been deputised to cover the annual Armistice Service but privately had arranged to spend the day walking in the dales with a favourite girl friend. There was a detailed printed programme of the Armistice proceedings which had never altered for the past fifty years, so I thought it safe enough to write a somewhat lively and imaginative account of the ceremony several hours before it took place – and went off for my walk. On my return I handed in my copy and went home – only to find out, from a subsequent carpeting, that because of bad weather the day's events had been considerably altered, so that my account was woefully inaccurate.

The other disaster was equally galling to the paper's editor since it resulted in the edition being delayed several hours. I had been sent to report on a big Agricultural Show, and part of my job was to copy out each of the contest results – a boy on a motor bike rushed these back to the newspaper offices for printing. At the end of a long and exhausting day I returned to headquarters feeling rather pleased with myself – to find lights blazing and the main offices still open – and awaiting me a deputation of the editor, assistant editor and news editor. One of them brandished before me a huge batch of my copy.

'What the hell's the meaning of this, Baker? Are you trying to be funny or what?'

'Why, what's wrong,' I said innocently.

'It's your handwriting that's wrong – it's so bad that none of the comps have been able to read a word – and we've got a blank page waiting to be filled.'

Crestfallen I had to go round at once to the home of the show secretary and obtain from him an approved list of results, typewritten this time.

It wasn't then that I was sacked from the *Telegraph* – well, I was never actually sacked, merely told I would do better to try my luck in Fleet Street – and in fact I spent two rather happy years at Derby, learning to savour the delights of the 'in' world of journalists, feeling very proud of myself when the chief sub or even the news editor bade me accompany him to the pub round the corner for a 'noggin'. Drink was, it often seemed, to be the be all and end all of our existence on the *Telegraph*, perhaps necessary to enable us to maintain such a hard slog of work. A lot of it came free, too – the manager of the local theatre was always careful to see I got a couple of large whiskies, for instance, in order to soften my impending review of the week's new show.

I suppose it would be fair to say that I got my true grounding in writing during my years on the *Derby Telegraph* (later on *Advertiser's Weekly* in Fleet Street). I learned that even an opening paragraph was dispensable, invariably being too flowery. I learned to appreciate the value of short sentences, even of short paragraphs – and to use one word rather than two wherever possible. Above all I learned the importance of capturing your reader's attention in the first few lines – otherwise the battle is lost.

I wish I had kept some of my early efforts. I can remember with some affection a series of articles on *Walks Around Derby* – also, with considerable amusement, another series on *Grand Old Men of Derbyshire*, in which every week I interviewed some octogenarian. I used to go to the local post office and ask for the address of the village's oldest inhabitant. Almost always the old men were real characters, often bizarre, – one I remember was seated in his outside loo and insisted on my interviewing him there and then!

One way and another my world of journalism was a lively and entertaining one, to which I gave myself wholeheartedly. During my six years in journalism I hardly seemed to have an outside life, the inside one was too absorbing. Looking back I do not think this was a bad thing, for I learned a great deal about human nature which might otherwise have remained a blank to me. Oddly enough I always found difficulty in recapturing it in my own writing. For many years I kept starting work on a 'great novel' about journalism – I can remember I had a marvellous opening scene of the young cub reporter driving down into the 'dark satanic mills' of the provincial town where he is to begin work. I had lots of vague details worked out, but somehow I always got stuck, and I never did complete the novel – unlike *Barbican's End*, which I took up after nearly thirty years and carried through to (I hope) a successful conclusion.

After Wales and journalism I suppose the war represents the next in my line of self-contained worlds. The war crystallised many of my views, helped to strengthen my strongly pacifist outlook, turned me finally into the vegetarian I have remained ever since. It also, by chance, led me to Youth House, that unique establishment where, despite the war, I spent three of the happiest years of my life. In Youth House – a pacifist and vegetarian community – I felt truly part of a large family of like-minded people. It was a large rambling old house on Camden Road, not far from Camden Town Tube Station, and the centre of some of the worst bombing raids of the war. Each of us had a small bed sitting room, and in the basement there was a restaurant – above that a large clubroom where we used to hold meetings and social functions.

As can be imagined with such a collection of forward thinking people we led a lively and interesting life, but we were not merely escapers from reality. Every evening we used to take huge pans of hot soup down to Camden Tube Station to distribute among families sheltering down there – also every Saturday we used to parade up and down Camden High Street selling *Peace News*, and invariably being engaged in heated discussions about our war views.

The blitz in London was something that just had to be experienced to be understood. Waiting for the sirens to sound, the planes to come, was just as emotionally upsetting as the actual raids when they came – as of course they did, night after night after night. Every morning it seemed my bus to work had to take a new route and columns of smoke could still be seen rising from the night's bombings. By a miracle Youth House was never hit but there were many bombs all around us, and the long Camden Road was soon pitholed with yawning craters. Shrapnel was always a danger – I can remember often walking home at night and dodging around as the metal pieces fell on the pavements around.

What a mad, mad world it all was. Little wonder that, at Youth House, we felt the need to cultivate still more strongly the movement towards a community life – a subject which, thanks to the war's impetus, continued to fascinate me. Indeed from Youth House I moved to a series of pacifist communities, savouring at first hand the problems of this way of life. Curiously enough it is often the small things and not the large ones that cause communities to break down – I can remember that when later on I was living with my first wife, Pat, at the White House Community led by an old man called 'Nunc' the final cause of the break up was a heated argument about who had been taking an unfair amount of the butter ration!

My next secret world that comes to mind was one I entered quite by chance some years after the war, when my first marriage had broken up and I was at a loose end. I saw an advertisement for help needed in starting a repertory theatre in Cornwall, wrote off immediately and was welcomed down to Camborne, along with my new girlfriend, Marie, a budding actress. I had no particular wish to act but imagined my writing skills could be used for publicity purposes, and this is what happened. Soon I was totally immersed in a fascinating new world, in which – just as at Youth House – we were so occupied with internal events that we hardly noticed the outside world. At Camborne, and later at Falmouth when I joined the Avon Players, a rather larger company, I met real 'pros' in the profession and picked up all the familiar theatre jargon – everyone is called 'darling', and things will be all right on the night and so on and so forth.

At both reps the programme was a series of weekly plays, and that way I learned to be familiar with *While Parents Sleep, Private Lives, Gaslight, Jane Eyre*, etc. As on the newspaper, one of the attractions of this new world was the 'in' side of being one of the gang so to speak. After performances, for instance, it was fun to sit around the deserted stage exchanging our reminiscences and experiences, bathed in the warm glow of fellowship.

While I was at the Avon Players the company made regular tours round Cornwall and whenever possible I would hitch a ride in the theatre van. It was always exciting to arrive at some town and start unloading the scenery and to be aware, as one did so, of the interest and curiosity of the local people. I suppose that is part of the pleasure of being part of a secret world – the knowledge that others may be envying one's unknown life. Life in the theatre, like life on a newspaper, was a hard one, but it had many rewards for which I have been eternally grateful.

My experiences at Camborne and Falmouth first drew me into the Cornish orbit – from then on I was trapped forever! This brings me to another of my secret worlds, which I experienced when I first went to live at my little Barn Cottage in the Penwith Hills above St Ives. Those were the years of the late 40's and early 50's when 'it was all happening' at St Ives – the town was full of young painters, many of them back from the wars, and all experimenting – Peter Lanyon, Bryan Wynter, David Haughton, Willy Barns Graham, Sven Berlin, Misome Peile.

It was an exciting and lively time to have been in St Ives. Each day I used to drive down into the town and savour its marvellous almost continental atmosphere. The winding cobbled streets were not only full of colour, but also it always seemed of dozens of friends among the artists and writers. Indeed it was often difficult to make much progress through the town without several enforced, and I must say very pleasant stops – at the second-hand bookshop run by Bill Barnes, for instance – at the Castle pub run by Endell Mitchell, brother of painter Denis Mitchell – or finally at the Sloop, the famous pub set on the edge of the harbour with a breathtaking view. Undoubtedly one of the main reasons for the pub's fame was through its association with the local artists. There were stories that more than one painting had often been presented to the landlord to 'clear the slate'. At the time of my arrival the walls were hung with a series of caricatures of local residents by Harry Rowntree – later these were replaced by drawings of local fishermen by Hyman Segal.

These were the times of the division of the artists between the old traditionals like John Park, with their big old-fashioned

New Gallery, and the new Penwith Society of Artists with their purpose-built modern new gallery off Back Road West – among their members such illustrious names as Ben Nicholson and Barbara Hepworth. Naturally enough I was drawn to the new breed of artists with their exciting new ideas. This is how one of the abstract artists, John Wells, put it:

> So all around the morning air and the sea's blue light, with points of diamond and the gorse incandescent beyond the trees; countless rocks, ragged or round and of every colour, birds resting or flying and the sense of a multitude of creatures living out their minute lives. All this is part of one's life and I was desperately eager to express it; not just what I see but what I feel about it and beyond it ... But how can one paint the warmth of the sun, the sound of the sea, the journey of a beetle across a rock, or thoughts of one's own whence and whither? That's one argument for abstraction. One absorbs all these feelings and ideas; if one is lucky they undergo an alchemistic transformation into gold and that is the creative work.

Many of the younger artists had rented old fish cellars and lofts and converted them into studios, and I remember with affection many lively afternoons in such picturesque surroundings. Later on, of course, our whole family were to live on the edge of Porthmeor Beach in St Christopher's, with its long low room opening out on to the booming surf – ah, magical times. Even now in my early years in St Ives many of the artists had studios looking out on that same beach and many were the parties that ended up with everyone running out for some enlivening midnight swim.

The Island was a particular mecca for the artists. Here Sven Berlin, the sculptor, had his studio and could be found working out in the open on some massive piece of granite. Several craftsmen set up on the island, too – notably Guido Morris the printer who left this memory of his beginnings:

> I was lucky enough to find a large empty room on the edge of the sea, what is called a net loft; in mine nets had actually been made until a few years before. I installed myself in one corner; brought in a few large tables, a single chair, and a safe; and built myself an elaborate system of bookshelves and pigeonholes for papers out of margarine boxes hoarded from before the war. I had gas installed but for the first year I fetched water in buckets from my nearest neighbour's cottage ... Into this place I finally arranged my 'iron soul', my Albion Press together with some three tons of impedimenta and a few hundred books, and I was in business.

So excited and stimulated was I by all these artistic goings on that I conceived the idea of starting a regional arts magazine, the *Cornish Review*. There seemed so much to record, indeed I was mystified that no one had had the enterprise to start such a magazine before then. Well I was going to change all that. I was going to bring out a magazine which would 'fulfil an obvious need – to provide a platform for discussing and analysing cultural activities in Cornwall, along with an outlet for new poetry and fiction by writers of Cornish descent or living in Cornwall'. What's more I would make it a proper job, no half measures but a magazine which any bookstall would be proud to display. A prospectus was drawn up and printed and for night after night Jess and I sat by the oil lamp in our little cottage folding up leaflets and inserting them in envelopes addressed to a variety of Cornwall lovers both at home and far afield.

I have written about the *Cornish Review* in earlier autobiographies so will not repeat myself here – I just wanted to bring it in as a further example of the general excitement of living in a budding art colony. I have long since left St Ives – and indeed the town has been sadly depleted of artists and seems given over now to Ye Olde Gifte Shoppes and fish and chip bars – but I shall always be grateful for that golden earlier era when living there was truly a magical experience.

Some years after St Ives I was to enjoy another secret and separate world – the world of *Sanu*, our dear old boat which we acquired with a legacy from my mother. Sixty feet by 18 feet by 7½ feet *Sanu* was an old Admiralty built MFV, and in her broad bosom we were to be carried off on many adventures – to Holland and Germany and Denmark and Sweden in the north, to France and Spain and Portugal and Italy and Greece and Turkey in the south. During some 20 years of cruising we experienced many traumatic moments (which I have described in *A Family at Sea*) and these are part of what constitute the important ingredients of this particular world. But when I think back now what I like to remember, in particular, are more the sheer delights of being able to cruise around, with friends and family, in a boat of your own. There's nothing like it. I mean to say – well let me haul up a few memories from the deep.

Well, of course, right away there's a quandary, for with a boat like *Sanu*, so stout and roomy and able to hold a dozen people in comfort, there's so much to remember. All those marvellous meals at the long table in the stern, under the stars, perhaps with a full moon hovering over the mast-head, other boats' anchor lights rocking gently around us – bliss, sheer bliss. How can one ever forget such occasions, even if they do tend to merge into one enormous symbolical portrait of a hundred such events? Cooking was always held in high regard aboard *Sanu* and we worked to a strict rota system, two unfortunate beings condemned to one day of misery and hard work – what's more expected to produce a gourmet meal, and in nine cases out of ten doing so. All this on the same small Calor gas stove inherited with the boat, powered since then by an amazing range of French, Spanish, Italian, Greek and Turkish gas cylinders (every one, needless to say, having different measurements).

It is difficult to pick out specific meals, but let's try. I shall always have a fond memory of *Sanu* tucked snugly between Ile Honorat and St Marguerite's, off Cannes, when our daughter

Gill served up a superb meal of red mullet in wine: and then, what a contrast, the one and only time we entered Port de Monaco with two slaves furiously preparing our evening meal – just as it was triumphantly brought on deck all the lights of Monte Carlo went out and then, as we still looked around in bewilderment, abruptly the sky was lit up by a most amazing firework display – in our honour of course we decided!

And then there was the memorable birthday luncheon at the lovely port of Marmaris in Southern Turkey where under the influence of some exceedingly cheap and potent Turkish pink champagne we ended up dancing a conga round and round the decks, joined in before long by several amused Turkish onlookers.

It was in Turkey that *Sanu* and her crew enjoyed perhaps our most spectacular of all anchorages – in the shimmering sky-blue waters of Ulu Deniz, an almost totally enclosed lagoon near Fetiye entered by a narrow neck between two beaches, with the towering 6,000 feet high Taurus mountains forming a suitably breathtaking background. Anchorages, indeed, have played an important part in *Sanu*'s history and although Ulu Deniz may gain the ultimate award there are many worthy contenders – like our privileged perch off Santorini nestling in the hollow between towering cliffs of what we at least became convinced had most claims to be the original of the lost land of Atlantis – like swinging idly in the sheltered wooded enclosures of Kalami Bay, Corfu, within a stone's throw of the villa where writers Lawrence and Gerald Durrell spent a charmed childhood – or, nearer home, almost any of our anchorages during a voyage round the Western Isles of Scotland, from the silent and beautiful waters of mountainous Loch Duich to the romantic history-laden setting of Dunvegan on the Isle of Skye, home of Dame Flora Macleod.

Then again, though they were berths rather than anchorages, we will always remember the unique experiences of that week at Port de Plaisance on the River Seine in the very heart of Paris, just a short walk from the Champs Elysées, and a similar sojourn along a leafy part of the canal right in the centre of Amsterdam, with all its gay life ... nor can I omit from this litany the memory of travelling some 350 miles through the Gota Canal, from Gothenberg to Stockholm, a journey encompassing 58 locks plus a couple of the largest lakes in Europe (one 2,123 square miles in area).

For me personally anchoring and berthing, the excitement of entering new ports were really the best part of having a boat of your own. I loved bringing *Sanu* into some totally strange port, finding a berth, then relaxing with a drink before (our usual custom in each new place) venturing out to enjoy a meal at some local restaurant – followed, the next day, by some inland exploration on the lines of two memorable examples, at Port Vecchio in Corsica, and again at Hania in Crete, where in both cases we hired mopeds and zoomed off on 60 mile trips up into the majestic mountains. However I was not blind to the more subtle pleasures to be derived from travelling as well as arriving and – like I am sure every other seasoned yachtsman – I remember with immense pleasure all those marvellous sunny calm days when the boat glided effortlessly through velvet seas, the sun riding high, perhaps one or two yachts bent their white sails gracefully on the horizon – and maybe, with a bit of luck, we were joined for a while by dolphins playing fast and seemingly dangerous games around our bow.

Yes, I have been fortunate indeed in having been able to enjoy so many different worlds – all of them fascinating and rewarding, though none of course quite measuring up to the marvellous ever-present one of our family life itself. Long may it continue –

VI

The Fortunate Isles

For more than thirty years our family has carried on a passionate love affair with the Scilly Isles: to this day every year sees Martin taking a holiday on St Martin's, while Gill and Alan and their children like to go camping at St Mary's, and other members of the family at the very least make day trips on the *Scillonian.* Only a couple of weeks ago there was quite a large expedition – Genevieve and Megan, Stephen and Gina and Paris and Armira, Gill and Alan and Amber and Cherry – all returning tired but triumphant, some of them bearing precious cuttings and plants to be put into our gardens at the Mill.

For Jess and myself it all began, as I say, some thirty years ago at a time when we lived above Sennen Cove in an old granite cottage exposed to wild winds from the west. You could not see the Scilly Isles from the cottage but it only required a short walk along the clifftops towards Land's End and there they were – a series of mysterious humps on the horizon, some thirty miles distant as the crow flies. From the beginning I was fascinated and intrigued at this glimpse of what must surely be some sort of paradise ... even the vast expanse of sea in between acquired a lustre of its own, for was it not below its waves that there lay the fabled lost land of Lyonesse? (I think this must have been the period when I clarified many of my ideas for my novel *Barbican's End* about a Cornish seaside village that disappeared into the sea one wild and stormy night.) Oh, yes, I can remember Jess and myself spending many delightful hours lying on the soft mossy turf of the cliffs and staring out to the golden horizon and all those craggy islands – the Fortunate Isles as one commentator aptly named them.

After falling in love with the Scillies from a distance it was to be some years before we finally made our personal acquaintance – and then it was in the best possible style, a voyage across in our own boat, our old *Sanu*. We set sail from Newlyn, following the last few miles of the South Cornish coast, past the stark outline of the Logan Rock, past the clearly visible outline of the open air Minack Theatre hewn out of the cliffs – finally past the hooting Runnelstone buoy and the storm cones kept above little Porthgwarra Cove – out into the open seas. Using the eight mile distant Wolf Lighthouse as a landmark we kept on a steady course and soon saw the outline of the isles ahead of us, St Mary's, the largest, beginning to unfold. Five hours after leaving Newlyn we were safely tied up at the stone harbour wall at St Mary's, eager to begin our explorations.

And what explorations there were! Because the islands are all so close together and the waters generally so shallow we used to leave *Sanu* tied up at the harbour and pile into our two large dinghies and zoom off – perhaps to take a look at St Agnes with its adjoining smaller isle of Gugh, perhaps to investigate Bryher and the magical sandy island of Sampson, perhaps to venture right across to St Martin's, the most northerly of the isles – more likely, though, to drop in at Tresco, next biggest to St Mary's, home of the Dorrien Smith family and a veritable paradise with its lush tropical gardens. At Tresco it seems to me there is everything – not merely tropical gardens, but a marvellous museum of ship's heads, Valhalla – glorious long deserted white sandy beaches as well as some fascinating moorland walks leading down to such intriguing historical centres as King Charles's Castle – and then, of course, a homely old pub in the New Inn, just above New Grimsby Quay.

In those early days we used to have with us Doug Rowe, a professional skin diver interested in finding buried treasures, and under his directions we used to anchor *Sanu* in the strait between Tresco and Bryher so that he could embark on some of his expeditions. We never found any treasures then but later Doug was lucky and was one of the group led by Rowland Morris who found the wreck of the *Association*, flagship of the famous Admiral Cloudsley Shovell – a wreck almost full to the brim with gold coins and other treasures. Personally I was never bothered much about the treasure-hunting – for me it was bliss enough to sit on *Sanu*'s deck as she swung idly at anchor, under what seemed endless sunshine and blue skies, listening to the seagulls calling, completely relaxed.

Because I assumed that this anchorage, just below Hangman's Isle, was a safe and protected one I used to use it in later years – a habit which, alas, was to lead in the end to the disaster I describe in *A Family at Sea*, when in the course of 'a quiet weekend on the Scillies' our beloved boat dragged her anchor and went on to the rocks and we had to be rescued by the St Mary's Lifeboat under Cox Matt Lethbridge. This was a time when perhaps our feelings towards the islands suffered a temporary setback – although even then I can remember gratefully how kind everyone was in helping us in our hour of need.

Sanu was almost a write-off and it required the full insurance plus some of our own money to cover her being raised from the depths, patched up at the St Mary's boatyard, then being towed over to Falmouth for extensive repairs. However in the end all was well, and *Sanu* lived to sail a good many years, and to venture much further afield than the Scillies to France and Spain, Italy and Greece and Turkey ... Somehow, though, we could never bring ourselves to sail her back to the Scillies. This did not mean any diminishing in our love for the islands – merely an indication of a strongly supernatural belief that it might not be wise to tempt providence.

Just what is it that is so fascinating about the Scillies? The very name is a cause for intrigue. One historian, Molly Mortimer, has suggested that it might be the old Cornish word for 'conger' or 'Sullea', the rock dedicated to the sun. One wonders ... Were these indeed the Cassiterrides, the tin islands of the Ancients, the Isles of the Blest, the Islands of the Dead? Did Jesus really visit them during the silent years? Were they the last resting place of the Norse King Olaf Trygvasson? Did Arthur's knights flee there after the last battle with Mordred, Tristram meet Iseult on Sampson? As Molly Mortimer has said, the aesthetic as well as the antiquarian eye can find a complete satisfaction. The Scillies are in fact a hundred isles, a thousand rocks where the peacock shoals are always laced with foam and the water is coloured like the crystals that lie on the shore: jade, chalcedony, amethyst, and topaz. Perhaps nowhere else could one find such conjunction of north and south. The seal and the porpoise watch the shark and the dolphin. The hardy northern guillemot rests on rusting palms. Outside the tropical gardens of Tresco lie uplands of heather and bracken, trees stunted by gales – yet one can light a fire with geranium and rosemary faggots, so high do these shrubs grow. Washed by the Gulf Stream it is nevertheless a most temperate climate where no snakes or other poisonous reptiles exist.

The history books have much to tell us about the Scillies. They were, it seems, once venerated as a burial place of the ancients. However religion as a major occupation has disappeared as has tin, whether Scilly were a mining centre, or merely a marketing place, which enabled foreigners to escape mainland dues. Agriculture and seamanship, both mentioned by the ancients, Strabo and Avenius, as highly developed in Scilly, have remained though in a changed form. Scillonian sheep, and the industries attached to wool have vanished with the coming of flowers, for the animals break into the flower patches and do more damage than their own worth. Throughout history fishing seems to have remained as the essential reserve industry, coming to the fore only in bad times.

And after the fall of Rome the Dark Ages were very dark in Scilly. The few scraps of information that have come down through Church records and the public Rolls indicate this. Indeed, as late as the time of Henry VIII, his surveyor Leland, observes: 'there be few men willing to inhabit these Islands for all the plentie, for robbers by sea take their catail of force.' Scilly remained a happy hunting ground for pirates and robbers through the Elizabethan era, when the Lord High Admiral of England himself was executed for piracy, centred round these islands.

After the Armada and the Civil War (Scilly was the last Royalist outpost) life gradually improved. Eighteenth-century writers give a pleasant picture of life on Scilly, and of its prosperity, perhaps increased by the garrison of some six hundred men in Star Castle. Borlase describes the plentiful crops and fruit. Troutbeck observes that even the poorest need never go in need of fish, barley, bread and potatoes. He lists a formidable number of trades flourishing on St Mary's: not only butcher, baker, brewer, cooper, weaver, tailor and mantua maker, but shipwrights and carpenters, joiners, masons, smiths, glaziers and barbers. Charity largely revived the fishing industry by the gifts of fish cellars, boats and tackle, and by the eighteen sixties, Scilly had become the headquarters of western mackerel fishing.

Meanwhile, on land, the rise and fall of one major occupation after another would make a fascinating study for the economic historian. Gone now, are the straw plaiters, the rope makers, reed thatchers, woolcombers, spinsters, hat and corset makers. The kelp, potato, shipbuilding and brewery industries have vanished with the twenty-three inns they supported on St Mary's. Gone is the garrison with the social milieu and the economic need it created. Kelp-making was originally brought to the Scillies so the tradition runs, by the Nances in 1784. It gradually became a widespread occupation and each family staked out its claim to special rocks for fetching the precious weed. Indeed, the eighteenth-century court books are full of litigation between indignant islanders on the subject of oreweed poaching.

By the 1840's the trade had been lost to the Northern Isles and to Spain, but as if in amends for this, the story runs that in 1838, the master of a Spanish vessel gave a Scillonian lad some seed potatoes. They were found to grow quickly and well, so, faced with the destruction of the kelp trade, the adaptable Scillonian turned to a new and highly profitable occupation. But by the end of the fifties England had become a Free Trade country, and the potatoes went the way of kelp, to Spain.

The amphibious Scillonian turned once again to the sea, and a swift and amazing development in shipbuilding took place. There are no records of the beginnings of this trade, of how the amateur, and every Scillonian wants to build his own boat, turned professional. But by the 1860's it was in full swing. The early boats were small because of the heavy dues to be paid on those over sixty tons, but Scillonian fifty-niners became world famous, and many a Scillonian crossed the Atlantic in a boat made on his front doorstep. As wood and wind gave way to steam and iron, shipbuilding and all the associated trades began to fail, in particular, the time honoured one of Channel Pilot. Time was, in the eighteenth century, when an easterly gale would fill the Roads with three hundred ships or more, and the whole Prussian fleet sheltered and re-victualled there in 1870. Pilots patrolled from Ushant to the Smalls, prowling in fierce competition for any ship that showed up from the west with her jack flying. In the sixties, there were ten pilot boats with eight men to each. Now there are only three pilots left, and those elderly.

Like the heroine of a thriller, the Scillies were once more snatched from disaster by the providential advent of the flower trade. William Trevellick collected 'lilies', especially Scilly Whites. The 'Governor' of the Island, who saw disaster coming, sent the famous hatbox of flowers to Covent Garden and received one pound for them. Thus was born the great industry of today, which has brought Scilly greater prosperity and skill than ever before.

*

During our many visits to the Scillies we often used to wonder what it would be like to actually live on the islands. Indeed it is my own guess that if we had come upon the islands at the beginning of our family life we might well have settled there. When I was running the *Cornish Review*, some years ago now, I went out of my way to publish several articles which helped to answer my own curiosity. Here for instance is a contemporary account we had from Helen May:

'The boat lurches and crashes amid the heavy sea. The breakers come flying over the bows and from the port side, and the little group of people huddled together under the comparative shelter of the wheelhouse discover ruefully that the water has found its way somehow down their necks and inside their oilskins. A fishing trawler at work? Perhaps a lighthouse relief party? No, simply the wintertime homeward trip to Tresco after completing the weekend shopping on St Mary's, in the Isles of Scilly. This is the scene after the hot summer days are gone, taking with them the familiar stream of visitors; and the nucleus, the residents, are left alone to enjoy these islands which present a very different face during the winter months, but still retain their fatal fascination for those who had fallen under their spell.

'Winter time is difficult by mainland standards, but the Islanders let events run their natural course, as is their wont, and are not unduly surprised or inconvenienced by the occasional hazards of day to day living which sometimes befall them. The failure of the steamer RMVS *Scillonian* to arrive because of appalling weather conditions means the non-arrival of all essentials. But while it is a focal talking point, there is no room for dismay; this is one of the happenings which the Islanders will take in their stride, which begins to explain their deeply ingrained independence; so at times like these the housewives bake home made bread and scones in their Rayburns, and it's "Just one of those things" that the post doesn't arrive. As for newspapers, no one will miss *them* – even in summertime the newspapers are unavoidably late in arriving; it generally raises a smile when delivery of the papers on the mainland is late, owing to one or other strike, it is sufficiently serious to be an item of national news; here the Sunday papers may come on Tuesday evening!'

Scillonian women don't expect the modern luxuries most of us almost take for granted. Not for them the convenience of throwing the family wash into the washing machine. A launderette on St Mary's might be expected to do booming business, but is non-existent, presumably on account of the limited water supply. So while the hotels and guesthouses pile their laundry basket off to Penzance, the average Islander is practically reduced to banging the clothes with a stone, and drying them with her hair-dryer! Helen May's visiting relatives found it an experience never to be forgotten – helping to grapple with sheets and blankets in an effort to overcome the elements and peg the blessed things on the clothes line in the garden.

There are no resident policemen on the off-islands; likewise the doctor, dentist and veterinary surgeon are based on St Mary's, as is the comparatively new, and much admired hospital. Thus an expectant mother either goes down weeks in advance of the delivery date, because of the tides, or offers up prayers that the boat will get her there in time. The boatman shares her prayers!

Television has been a welcome innovation into Island homes, and reception is now further enhanced by the booster on St Mary's. There is a cinema, too! With a sparse informal group sitting around it's more like a family privately viewing TV. The pictures are shown in the Reading Room, where most of the Island communal activities are held.

'For the most part the cottage Rayburns are fed with wood, so "wooding" is an occupation nearly everyone pursues diligently. Apart from the plentiful driftwood to be found along the most beautiful beaches, the Island is thickly wooded with pine trees, and the cones and fallen wood to be found therein mostly provide the answer to the fuel problem. The services of a milkman, in the conventional sense, don't exist. Each family takes its empty milk can to the farm as an evening ritual, and collects the required number of pints the next day. It may mean a half-mile walk each way, but you soon take that in your stride!

'Off season, in the absence of the visitors, the islands are still busy, for it is now that the flower industry comes into its own. Before Christmas every available pair of hands is concentrating upon the flower output. The pickers have an unenviable task. To the uninitiated it sometimes raises an image of leisurely plucking of blooms under a blue sky and smiling sun. In fact, of course, when the buds are suitably developed the beds are picked speedily, come wind, come weather. A force 10 gale may rip through the fields, bringing with it driving, blinding rain, but the flowers still have to catch the market; and there are a good few aching backs and stiff limbs at the end of the day. Tractorloads of differing varieties arrive at cottage doors, and here it is that the womenfolk take over the cutting and bunching, the preparation necessary before the flowers can begin their journey to markets on the mainland.

'But the kinder weather soon returns, the sun smiling a foretaste of summer. The hotels and guesthouses make their early start to the long season, and in February the first visitors filter through a holiday paradise devoid of traffic, fumes and the usual bustle of modern civilisation. The cottages of fishermen and farmers open to welcome visitors for their stay, and the harbours and bays fill with small craft and yachts. In the settled weather the calmer seas will afford enjoyable boat trips to inhabited and uninhabited islands, as well as to see seals, and such events as the relief of the Bishop Rock Lighthouse – a spectacular event usually executed by pulleys. The brawny boatmen look as though they might have stepped out of time, with their weather-beaten, leathery brown faces and beards of biblical proportions. Occasionally impatient of visiting boats, but always ready to lend a steadying hand to the landlubbers boarding their tripper boats.

'Even through the heavenly summer months, the trip to St Mary's can be quite an experience! At low tides, when the boats cannot moor alongside the quay, they wait offshore while women with babies, pushchairs and shopping baskets scramble over rocks, seaweed and wet sand, sometimes splashing through puddles an inch or two deep to reach the water's edge. Holidaymakers are in the same boat with quantities of luggage. If they're lucky, there's a small punt to ferry them out in relays to the waiting boat; otherwise decorum is flung to the winds as the boatman in his waders carries women and children across the stretch of water, and unsuitably clad men receive a piggyback!

'For an Islander, a trip to a nearby uninhabited island is always fraught with interest. And apart from anything else, it's a retreat from the crowds! So their punt, catamaran or whatever is pulled down the beach and Tresco is left behind for a short while. Especially worthwhile is a trip like this to see gulls' eggs and newly-hatched youngsters. Beachcombing may be especially rewarding, too. A chart from the ill-fated Poleire figures prominently in a local collection. On the return journey there are lobster pots to be attended to, and with any luck a catch to put in the bottom of the boat. Then it's homeward bound. Tresco is coming closer again, the red sun setting on the one hand, and the moon rising, pale and hazy, on the other. It's very quiet, and the water holds many reflections. The coloured lights of Tresco's Island Hotel wink a friendly invitation as the boat purrs past Northwethel.'

Entertainment is the home-made variety, and the pub rings to lusty sea shanties. Different nationalities seem drawn to Scilly, and when visiting French leave their yachts to join the singing in the pub, the locals are only too pleased to give their best rendering of 'Alouette', 'Frère Jacques' and anything else remembered from schooltime French! Summer barbecues are very popular – though, of course, they may only commence *after* closing time – and hot dogs and folk singing get under way. Flames leap into the warm summer night and silhouettes sit cross-legged on the sand, or dance to a guitar. It's well into the early hours when it breaks up. The fire is dwindling, and someone shouts for the St Martin's contingent to depart. Quick 'goodnights' are exchanged and so many shapes tread noiselessly down the beach into darkness. There are the faint sounds of casting off, and then their oars splash away into the night. Soon the others have put out the fire and drifted away in twos and threes. Until the next time.

Inter-Island gig racing is popular and well supported. The crews practise several times a week and when Friday comes round everyone is out to join the visitors and shout support for their team. Tresco and Bryher together man the 100-year old gig the *Czar*. The tripper boats follow the race, giving supporters a good view of the progress, or otherwise, of 'their' gig. The races mostly finish at St Mary's quay, and if you're lucky, and the wind and tide permit, you have an excuse for a night out in St Mary's; the boat leaving for the return trip at 11 p.m. with precious packets of fish and chips unobtainable on the off-islands. On an ebb tide maybe a boat is already tied up at New Grimsby quay, and the late night revellers are obliged either to scramble over the wheelhouse and across the moored boat to the quay, or abandon fancy footgear and leap onto the beach. Or maybe the tide dictates a return journey via the back of Bryher and into the channel from the north, putting everyone ashore below Cromwell's Castle, a landing not really advisable after a few hours spent in the Mermaid on St Mary's!

'Opening hours are sacred to the Scillonian. And who's to mind? No drinking and driving to worry about. It's a great life! Of course from time to time some mishap results – some happy fellow goes overboard or walks off the end of the quay – but all ends well!

'Some of the islands suffer acutely the same problem that exists on the Cornish mainland. Cottages are purchased by up-country people for holiday use only; so that they are occupied for a few weeks in the summer and stand empty for the remainder of the year. Young people who want to make Island homes are therefore prevented from doing so, and the resultant population decrease has become so serious that there is currently talk of depopulation. No one wants to be forced to leave their homes. No doubt they will be adamant that they should be allowed to stay. But how can such a very small area be expected to flourish while property is handled in this way?

The people are hardy and down-to-earth; they have to be. It's no easy business scratching a livelihood there, with precious few creature comforts, but they are proud of their heritage, and surely have every right to be. At least that was Helen May's opinion. The Scillies are wild, and cultivated; exposed, and sheltered; rugged, and soft. Such extremes of nature within so small an area need to be seen to be believed. What a wealth of colour, scenic beauty and fascination the Isles of Scilly provide!

A lively and personalised view of how entertaining life on the islands could be was once provided by Ronald Davies when he shared with us his youthful memories of inter-island cricket matches in an article in the *Cornish Review*:

'Matches played at home on St Agnes were one thing; matches played away were quite another. There was the little matter of getting to the other island, for one thing. The Scillonians knew the channels, the rocks and reefs, and the currents as well as most people know the familiar neighbourhood they live in. Getting from Agnes to Bryher, or Tresco, or to far-away St Martin's at the other end of the Isles, was no great matter in reasonable weather. But weather in Scilly is vilely unpredictable. Many a fair morning heralded in a Force Eight gale.

'A spell of fine weather usually meant the St Agnes team, on the most isolated island in Scilly, fixed up a match by telephone, and set off the next Sunday afternoon. It was the best of both worlds, aboard a boat on the way to another island to play cricket. There was all the pleasure of a sea-trip on a fine day, with the white beaches gleaming on the edges of the green islands, and a game of cricket to follow.

'One such afternoon the St Agnes team gathered on the old lifeboat launching slip at the back of the island looking out to the Western Rocks and the Bishop light. Israel Hicks was providing transport. His boat was the only one big enough to take the whole team. It was a palatial affair, with an enclosed cabin, and portholes. "Like the bleddy *Queen Mary*!" said some.

'Even I, no seaman at all, though I had been born so close to the sea that during the winter gales the waves hurled pebbles against the front of the house, thought she seemed to ride rather high out of the water. The cabin caught the wind like a sail. Even on the calm sea between the islands she seemed to rock quite a bit in only a light air.

'No matter; we got safely to Carn Near on Tresco. The tide was right out, so we anchored as close in as we could, and then ferried the team ashore in the punt in only two trips. The only way to do that was for everybody to stand up, which didn't make for stability or much freeboard, but saved making trips.

'We walked through the bracken up the sandy track to the cricket pitch, carrying all the well-worn gear. It was a beautiful afternoon. The sun shone; the ball hurtled through the air; the bat flashed in daring strokes; there were cries of "Ow zat?", catches were made with great dexterity; and dropped with an equal lack of it; runs were scored, batsmen run out – it was a lovely game of cricket on Tresco in the summer.

'Both teams took their tea in Valhalla, surveyed by the blind eyes of the figure-heads from wrecked ships. After the baking heat of the cricket field it was a cool green haven. The tea was proper provender for hungry cricketers; bread and delicious butter, cakes, saffron cake, and quarts of strong tea.

'It was a very English occasion, but neither the cricketers nor the island looked very English. With Tresco's exotic plants all around, the mahogany tans and weather-beaten faces could have been those of Captain Cook's men on some Pacific island. Perhaps more like Henry Morgan's crew ashore in the Caribbean, some might think. The blue agapanthus and scarlet fuchsia; the palms, the cacti; the sub-tropical palms, all added to the illusion. It was rather like being an extra in some film; a feeling I often had in Scilly.

'The after-tea innings were memorable for me because I hit a boundary off the first ball. Only the undeniable fact that I looked the other way when I did it marred the feat. Certainly it was not my intention to send it the way it went. I was quite surprised to hit it at all. However, the next ball clean bowled me, and I was glad to go and sit with the very few remaining batsmen. It felt safer sitting on the grass close to the scorer. Nobody was going to shy cricket balls at him.

'The sky was clouding over I noticed, and a few little gusty breezes hinted the wind might be getting up. Now and then a bit of scud flitted by. It seemed a good idea to be setting off to Agnes. There was the evening milking to do, and all the other jobs that make life more comfortable on one of the off-islands.

'Getting back to the boat was a repeat performance of the hair-raising business of landing, with about three-and-a-half inches of freeboard, and the bottom of the sea clearly visible twenty feet below the punt. Samuel Plimsoll would have gone to an early grave in Scilly. Probably a burial at sea.

'The weather was clearly getting worse as we headed out into the channel back to Agnes. The wind was freshening from the westward and the waves rising steeply. The light was wan and grey. The white beaches on the edges of the islands were barely visible. The top-heavy boat lurched sickeningly. Cold spray hit the face with a sharp sting that wasn't much like summer. But the boat thudded steadily towards the outline of the old lighthouse on the crest of Agnes. With any luck we would just get home before the gale came, and there was plainly going to be a gale.

'Without any warning there was a sudden grinding halt in the boat's steady course. Cricketers fell into the bottom-boards, cursing. Waves began to slop over the gunwales, soaking them as they struggled to get to their feet. We were fast on sand.

' "The waddeh no sandbank here last week!" a protesting voice said as the screw churned into reverse. But the boat stuck fast. The wind seemed stronger; the sea vaster and greyer. We were stuck on a sandbank somewhere between Tresco and Agnes, with a cricket team and all its gear aboard, and a gale on the way. And we hadn't even won the match. It seemed a miserable way to go.

'It didn't take long for the stranded cricketers to decide what to do. There was nothing for it but to get out and push. Over the side went the able-bodied men in the St Agnes team and heaved away at the boat. They were mostly up to their waists in the sea, and stood a good chance of floundering off the sandbank into deep water if the boat got clear. But that didn't stop them. It seemed a very long time indeed before the hull lifted clear, and the screw churned the boat free as the dripping cricketers scrambled aboard. By now we were all wet, more or less, but we were inboard, and the sea was a lot wetter.

'The wind assaulted the boat fiercely and the waves battered the hull as we headed for Agnes against the run of the tide. The danger would come when we were rounding the end of the island and were broadside on to the wind and the currents. It would be quite easy to run on to the rocks then, even though the men of Scilly are among the best seamen in the world.

'It was a chancy business, and we nearly found ourselves on the jagged reefs off Agnes more than once. The boat would have been smashed to pieces, and we would have had to take our slim chances swimming ashore if we could. More than once the helmsman put the bows into the wind and headed apparently for America to give himself some leeway before attempting to put in, but there was no sea-room among the reefs.

'All the time we were trying to make the cove we could see people standing on the old lifeboat slip. The crowd seemed to get bigger as time went on. When we finally thumped our way through the mazy, weedy channel into Periglis and the safety of the cove and the slip under the church most of the islanders seemed to be there.

'The cove felt safer and secure after our buffeting on the sea. Although we had never been out of sight of land we had been in as great peril as if we had been in the middle of the Atlantic. There would have been small hope of swimming to shore, and less of scrambling through the breaking waves over the rocks. Not all those aboard could swim, in any event. There is a strongly-held belief that the ability to swim only prolongs the agony if you fall overboard anywhere off Scilly. Some islanders had never learned to swim for that reason.

'Few cricket teams can have been in danger of drowning at sea on the way home after a match. Fewer can have had to get out and push after running their boat on to a sandbank. But it all added to the distinctive flavour of life in Scilly, where nothing is quite the same as the mainland.'

VII

My Personal A-Z

The other day I began playing a variation on the 'I spy' game – instead of declaring 'I spy something beginning with A' I decided to compile a veritable A-Z of some of my more interesting lifetime experiences. Beginning, naturally enough, with A.

A – well in my experience that can only stand for aeroplane, because of course my father was a famous flying instructor and through this fact I was early on brought into close contact with the flying world. My father was instructor at Stag Lane Aerodrome, later at Heston, and often he would take me with him to spend a day at the club – which meant, for me, wandering around and looking, often with awe, at some of the smart new planes of the day, the De Havilland Puss Moth, the Avro, the Piper and so forth. I was never quite able to share my father's huge enthusiasm but I could see the attraction and excitement about being able to soar up into the air like a bird. My father seemed to be doing this all day long, no sooner had he landed from giving one lesson than he was turning the plane round and bearing off yet another eager pupil.

Among the latter were many famous people – Amy Johnson, Lady Londonderry, the Duchess of Bedford, Hamish Hamilton, often the Prince of Wales and his brother the Duke of Kent. With them all my father had an easy *bonhomie* that reflected his immense popularity. So it was sad that I and my father always remained curiously apart. Indeed the main incident I remember from those aeroplane days serves to emphasise this apartness. One day my father took me up for a trip around and, very much against my wishes did a loop the loop which frightened me to death! However I gained my revenge when a little later the engine spluttered into silence and my father was obliged to make a hurried forced landing on the first available space, which happened to be Hurst Park Racecourse. This also happened to be only a mile from our home at East Molesey – so the moment the plane had come to a halt I resolutely climbed out of the cockpit, bid an unfriendly farewell to my father – and started walking home!

B – I suppose could be for Baker. A pretty common name really and one about which I know very little since for some reason the tagged on Val (which is really a Christian name) has always appeared to lift us up above the common herd. In the telephone directory there are hundreds of Bakers but only one Val Baker – or I should say two, since my daughter Demelza is now on the phone. Baker sounds a typically English name but in fact it is quite common in Wales, and from Wales I most definitely derive. So far as I know there has never been an actual baker in the family, but we all love good strong wholemeal bread, I must say. Searching among the well known I cannot find many supremely successful Bakers, but there were actors Stanley Baker and George Baker, as well as the naturalist Richard St Barbe Baker. And of course by coincidence my dear and best friend Frank Baker shared the same surname – indeed we used to play with the idea of writing books together under the pseudonym of Colenso Baker but that, alas, never came to fruition.

C – well this could only be Cornwall. Having lived in the county now for some 35 years I could be forgiven for thinking of myself as practically a native, but I have no illusions on this score. To the Cornish you are not a local until you and your family have been around for several centuries, and preferably have names like Tregonna or Hocking or Blewett or Trevithick. Fortunately it is not the Cornish that concern me so much as Cornwall the place. I must have written hundreds of thousands of words about Cornwall – in articles, talks, books – and yet I still feel I have not quite captured its mystery.

What I do know is that Cornwall is unique in Britain. It would be difficult to drum up much excitement 'going to Essex' or 'going to Leicestershire' yet to this day there remains an intangible yet very real romanticism about 'going to Cornwall'. It is going west, towards the sun, into the mysterious land of Lyonesse, another world. Cornwall is different, apart, solidly and unmistakably, and in the fullest geographical sense. Even its position of being the most westerly of all English counties at once puts it quite literally out on a limb. No other English county has such a long coastline – in no other county are even all the inland areas so close to the sea. Sea washed and impregnated in this unusual way then no wonder Cornwall seems a place apart – what I have called the haunted land. It is as a draughtsman's country that Cornwall makes its impact upon us: as a gaunt skeletal figure of stone, writhing and contorting into strange shapes, inhabiting a world of shadow and darkness where colour is neither present nor needed. In this bleakly defined form the county may be said to achieve a curious kind of unity – the open and treeless surroundings of Tintagel in the east, for instance, being similar to the bleakness of St Just-in-Penwith in the west, and both surrounded by the same wide prospect or sea. Even on the south coast, though woodlands are to be found up one or two estuaries there is the same pattern of windswept treeless lands, the same awareness of a grim reality of life, whether by land or sea. Wherever you go in Cornwall, indeed the more you travel about, the more the perceptive visitor must come to recognise that here indeed is a granite kingdom that is very much its own domain.

D – I think this must stand for my eldest daughter, Demelza – named, of course, after Winston Graham's heroine of the *Ross Poldark* novels. A free spirit if ever there was one, I like to think. A mass of contradictions, of course, full of fears and apprehensions but imbued by a natural gaiety and *joie de vivre* that communicates itself – not least in her musical talents. Unusually among females Demelza is a percussionist, an outstanding conga player, and has played with some of the best bands in the country in her time, when she did session work in London. More recently she has been featured with an Afro Rock band in Cornwall, Zambula. Demelza is hardly an intellectual – but she is very beautiful, and that makes up for a lot in life, I fancy. Now that she has her own little baby, Morgan, she seems to be rather more beautiful in a mature and mellow way. Along with her bright-eyed blonde younger sister Genevieve, Demelza has made me laugh and cry and jump for joy and be cast down with gloom – altogether life with her has never had a dull moment.

E – is for Earth. What a marvellous thing is our great planet which bears this rather ordinary name. Just think of the golden lands and the sea-blue seas – the mountains and the valleys – the rivers and the lakes. And so to F for fortunate – as we have been to have travelled a considerable amount. We in our family have truly come to appreciate the wonders of the earth we inhabit. Variety, endless variety, is the key to it all, so that on the one hand there are great cities like London and Paris and Rome with their teeming millions and their fascinating buildings – on the other hand still small spots of beauty like a remote part of the Cornish coast or the top of some wild Welsh mountain, or perhaps an extraordinary setting like Greek Santorini – the lost land of Atlantis to which we sailed one day aboard *Sanu*. Yes, the earth is surely worth its weight in gold – what a tragedy that we seem intent on destroying it as soon as we can. We must be mad indeed.

G – is for Genevieve, my other and younger daughter, in many ways a complete opposite to Demelza (though one of my secret delights has been the deep and loving bond that has always existed between them). Where Demelza is dark, Genevieve is blonde and rather ethereal-looking – a gentle and delicately sensitive creature with an underlying toughness which she has needed in a life which she has tended to lead very much on her own account. Stubborn to the nth degree (a typical Taurus) Genevieve has often been her own worst enemy. Possessed of a number of outstanding talents – in art, in music, in the esoteric – she has tinkered about with pursuing too many, whereas in my opinion if she had concentrated on a single direction she could have risen to the top.

In particular she has great artistic flair, and this emerges in the marvellously colourful and delicate pottery ware which she produces – great plates filled with breathtakingly beautiful illustrations – tiles covered with hauntingly beautiful images of white gods and princesses with flowing hair, dragons and saints and sinners ... Because she is so choosy Genevieve has not yet married or committed herself to any permanent relationship – still in her romantic way she is looking for that 'white knight' to come riding along – however, fortunately in all our opinions, she has managed to acquire a beautiful little daughter, Megan, a fact which has brought great joy not only to her but to myself as well. To see blonde Genevieve leading grave-faced blonde Megan along a country lane, picking spring flowers, is a joy to behold. Great love sweeps out from Genevieve and all around her beloved child, and that cannot be a bad thing.

One other thing – most of all my family Genevieve has taken after me in her love for the sea and has emulated me in a practical way by regularly attending navigational classes so that she can acquire her master's certificate, and therefore be equipped one day to go off on some round-the-world voyage. I shall be sad to see her and Megan go, but realise this is part of life's inevitable pattern.

H – is for Holidays. Ever since childhood days I have always found the idea an exciting one – to escape to somewhere new. One of my greatest pleasures too (and here perhaps I am lucky in having that sort of temperament) is in the preparations. During all our wonderful *Sanu* days I got tremendously excited in the winter months sitting by a roaring fire and plotting courses for our forthcoming summer cruises! And what holidays we have had, thanks very largely to *Sanu* – a trip through the Gota Canal, with its 58 locks – another river trip up the River Seine and into the heart of Paris – meanderings around the Greek Isles – wonderful, wonderful. Of course there have been other holidays, too. When I was very young the height of my holiday ambitions was to spend my time up at Llanfairfechan on the coast of North Wales – at a later stage I became interested in hiring boats and taking trips on the Llangollen Canal, on the Norfolk Broads, finally down Ireland's great thoroughfare, the River Shannon. A visit to the West Coast of Scotland provided one of our most unforgettable holidays – who could fail to be excited by islands like Mull and Skye (where we visited the late Dame Flora Macleod in her Dunvegan Castle).

Usually our holidays tend to have been family ones, but two I remember where Jess and I escaped on our own. Once, soon after winding up affairs after my mother's death, we booked passage on one of the big cruise liners and sailed from Venice around the coast of Yugoslavia and Greece and then up to Istanbul. I rather enjoyed being able to sit back and be waited on and we met some fascinating and bizarre people. And then there was Bermuda – not altogether a holiday since Jess was invited out there to help someone start a hand-made pottery – but we had lots of free time to explore the very beautiful 'Isles of Devils' as they were called in centuries past (because they were so remote and surrounded by treacherous reefs lurking just beneath the surface of the turquoise sea). Bermuda in fact is made up of 150 islands, the seven largest being inhabited and joined together by man-made causeways. The secret is to do what we did and hire mopeds, on which you can zoom around the tropical fish-hook shaped island.

Ah, those marvellous sunny days when we threaded our way down avenues lined with oleanders and bougainvilleas and morning glory and passion flowers, in the background the famous Bermudean cedar trees – ah, those fabulous beaches –

those pink coral reefs – those incredibly clear waters – those marvellous old schooners at their moorings in St George's – those mouth-watering bars and restaurants lining the waterside at Hamilton, the capital – Horseshoe Bay where on Sunday afternoons a gay calypso band would serenade one's Sunday afternoon siesta – and Ely Harbour where Jess and I boarded a glass bottomed boat and hovered, fascinated, over a coral reef watching all manner of colourful tropical fish, octopi, blue fish, lobsters, squid. Water, of course, was very much a part of daily life. Even an ordinary ferry boat crossing Hamilton Sound would be a great adventure for the boat would wind in and out among tiny islands dotted here and there with pink houses basking in sunshine. Perhaps our most remarkable day came at Easter when some friends took us out on their yacht to watch the famous annual race at St George's between half a dozen 14-foot Bermuda fitted dinghies which each carries more than 1,000 square feet of sail. To carry such a quantity of sail on such a small boat is a hazardous business and there were frequent spills. In addition it was accepted practice at difficult moments for crew members to jump *voluntarily* into the sea in order to lighten their craft! One way and another it was an entertaining day, ending with a candle-lit meal at Tom Moore's Tavern, a sort of pub-cum-restaurant whose walls were decorated with well known extracts from Tom Moore's poetry.

I – is for international – until we break down all the barriers and the world is a truly international place there is no hope for us. I have always disliked out and out nationalism – cultural nationalism yes, that's fair enough, but not any other variety. (Nazism was the supreme bad example.) All through my life I have felt in myself a natural spirit of internationalism, perhaps encouraged by my pacifism – and I have been glad to see the same spirit in the family. We do not know the meaning of racism or colour bars or other similar barriers – we like people for who and what they are, not the colour of their skin. Travelling around on *Sanu* helped a lot, of course, one soon learned that the world was full of people of all shapes and colours, and that they could all be equally pleasant or unpleasant – irrespective of their nationality. There are many things I do not like about the Common Market, but if it helps to do away with customs barriers and so forth, then good luck to it. I look forward quite simply to the day when there is just one United States – a United States of the World – in which we are all brothers together.

J is for Jess, my wife for the past 35 years. Our meeting was of the stuff that romances are made – 'You must meet this little Sagittarian,' said an astrological friend of mine. 'Just right for a Scorpio like you' – and how right he was! On the face of it no coupling could be more hazardous. Scorpions are dark and secretive and jealous – Sagittarians are open and honest and daredevil – yet in fact this very combination of opposite characteristics seems to work like a charm. For most of our lives Jess and I have argued and disagreed and blown up in rages at one another – but somehow never beyond a certain point, always underneath there has lurked that hidden, marvellous quality of lovingness, ready to emerge movingly with a certain look, a glint in the eyes, an unspoken awareness of what we were both really feeling.

It has helped, no doubt, that we had both previously experienced broken marriages, benefiting from learning from those earlier mistakes – and indeed when we got married we brought to our new relationship something else, too, for I had Martin with me and Jess already had Gill and Jane, so we started life together with a ready-made family. The coming of our own three children not only brought us great joy but undoubtedly deepened our love and affection tremendously.

As readers of my books should have comprehended by now, Jess is a remarkable woman – a truly independent and courageous spirit with immensely practical abilities. Gardening, pottery, motherhood, psychology, swimming – you name it, Jess will not only tackle it but make a success story as well. Some of her more casual acquaintances are a little put off, even frightened, by her sheer energy and determination – those who know her better are aware of all the endearing vulnerabilities behind those efforts, for basically Jess is a shy and gentle soul. When I first saw her framed in the doorway of a Fulham flat I felt a total flow of empathy and lovingness, and for most of our time together ours has been one of those marriages made in heaven as they say.

Sadly in the last few years my illness has made me difficult to live with and at times Jess grows weary of our routine life – but then, like a true Sagittarian she will escape for a week round the London theatres, or a holiday with a sister, at least a change – returning all smiles and happiness again. In some senses I may have been the adventurer of the family – but I would have been nothing without the rock firm heart of our loving family which Jess has always provided.

K – is for Kimbers, that small but enterprising firm of publishers which has brought out my books for the past fifteen years or so (and in doing so, I see, has produced no fewer than 25 works). It was a lucky day for me when I made the contract. What happened was that, sadly, my previous publisher, John Baker, died, leaving me without a publisher. I had just written a book about some of my *Sanu* adventures, under the rather good title of *The Petrified Mariner*. I looked through the pages of the *Writers and Artists Yearbook* and came across an entry under Kimbers stating that they published, among other things, books of nautical interest so sent in the book. To my pleasant surprise I got a fairly prompt acceptance, and the book was quickly brought out, excellently printed and with a gay coloured cover by Donald Swan showing an anxious captain Baker at the wheel of a storm-tossed *Sanu*. Had I any other books in mind, enquired Kimbers – so I sat down and wrote *An Old Mill by the Stream*, describing how our family came to leave the Old Sawmills and move down here – the book had an excellent sale, and suddenly we were in permanent business together.

Since then Kimbers have published twelve of my

autobiographies – they have also obliged and pleased me very much by bringing out a series of collections of my short stories as well as several novels. In all this they have maintained not only a high standard of production but also of author treatment and consideration. Nobody could have been kinder or more helpful than Peter Kimber and his fellow director Amy Myers, my two main contacts. Tall and distinguished, Peter came into publishing the hard way through a long and arduous apprenticeship at Hutchinson's – since striking out on his own he has kept resolutely to a middle path, bringing out good solid books with the occasional best seller, of which the best known must be *Exodus*.

My books are not anything like best sellers but they *are* steady sellers, and that is the basis on which Peter has built his very solid little empire – helped greatly by Amy Myers' flair for picking her way through the literary minefields. I was delighted a year or two back when it was announced that in a survey conducted by the Society of Authors among their members as to which firm was the most popular who should be top of the poll but Kimbers!

L – is for the literary world, or should I say literature. There is a difference – the first category can often be shallow and false, but the second is somehow permanent and true. Personally I have always quite enjoyed the literary world, especially attending those conferences of the Society of Authors and the West Country Writers Association, where there was a blessed chance to talk shop among one's fellow professionals. Writers lead rather lonely lives; it's good sometimes to mix in. Unlike some people I have never found writers particularly bitchy – certainly nothing so much as painters whose vanity and jealousies have often sickened me. Editing such a large number of anthologies as I have done has enabled me to meet writers of all kinds, and from all parts. Among my personal favourites have been Henry Williamson and Leo Walmsley, Winston Graham and Charles Causley, Derek Stanford and Fred Urquhart – and of course dear old Frank Baker.

Literature, now, that's a more serious subject. Literature is important as it is one of the cornerstones upon which our civilisation stands or falls. We in Britain have been fortunate in our great traditions of literature – after all, I suppose Shakespeare leads the world. For myself I am more interested in modern literature than the past, and I admire in particular the works of Graham Greene, John Fowles and Edna O'Brien among our present figures, Henry Williamson, Evelyn Waugh and Mary Renault among the immediate past. Great literature, even just good literature, can be recognised in the first page of reading, there is a quality that cannot be denied. So don't ever neglect good books – they can be some of your best friends.

M – must be for my eldest son, Martin, the product not of my second marriage, but of my first earlier marriage to Pat Johnson. I shall always have a soft spot for Martin, partly because he was my first child, partly because in so many ways he reminds me of myself – uncertain, apprehensive, self-effacing, diffident, etc. etc. Also he is a great tactician, another quality we share. In the early days of my second marriage Martin used to use his tactical skills to avoid rows with Jess, with whom now he gets on quite well. It must be said that of all the family Martin has kept most to himself, having some kind of inbuilt horror of being swamped by crowds of relatives (yet paradoxically he takes a keen interest in all the family goings on and keeps a family scrapbook). However one has to admire his independence, for he seeks desperately never to be beholden to anyone else and ever since he left art school has somehow often under considerable difficulties, kept himself going on his own account. Martin loves Cornwall deeply and has spent nearly all his life down in his favourite county. For a time he lived in London working for a wine firm, driving their delivery van all over the place – but as soon as he could he came down west, at first continuing the driving experience by working for a furniture firm – finally, and about time too, making use of his art school experiences to go into printing. For nearly ten years he worked for a Penzance firm and then finally set up on his own account – since when he has operated in a small untidy little workroom down an alley opposite Penzance Station. Here he not only prints but follows his own favourite occupation of being a musical entrepreneur, organising concerts down here by George Melly, the Barbara Thompson Band, Maddy Prior and many others.

Just as our youngest, Genevieve, has remained unattached, so has Martin, our eldest. Once he had a three-year great romantic affair with a marvellous girl and we all cheered, but alas in the end it broke up – now there are dangerous signs of him settling into severe bachelorhood, but I keep my fingers crossed in the hope that suddenly one day some new pretty (and intelligent) face will sweep him off his feet.

N – is for night, that reward to which we look forward as we labour through the long day. Night is the time when we gather with our children around the family hearth, or perhaps when we hold some celebratory meeting or dinner. I shall never regret such events as the night of our Twenty-Fifth Wedding Anniversary when we assembled twenty-five family and friends in our big kitchen at the Mill House and wined and dined until the early hours – nor the similar occasion of Jess's sixtieth birthday when we managed to collect a handful of her friends from earlier days and savoured her favourite meal of lobster thermidor.

Night can be romantic, too, walking under the stars with a loved one – particularly by the sea, with the moon glistening on the wild waters, creating a sort of magic. But then night can be a hard time, too, particularly later on in the rather fearful early hours, they say that the human spirit is at its lowest ebb between 2 a.m. and 3 a.m. and this I certainly know to be true! At such times one is darkly aware of death and destruction, of the complete negation of life that ultimately lies ahead. It can, too, so often be a time of terrible pain and unhappiness. Thank goodness in the end night is followed by day, glorious unknown, exciting new day.

O – is for the Old Sawmills, possibly our most romantic ever home during a third of a century of family life together. I have often described how Jess and I first saw that marvellous, indeed unique place. We left our car at Golant and set off walking along the old railway line that runs alongside the River Fowey. Suddenly, coming round a bend – there was the Old Sawmills, a large pink building set in its own creek. Of course it was high tide which showed everything off at its best but neither of us would ever forget that first view: the long stretch of calm water leading up to the tiny quays, rising above them a small chalet and then, nestling as if growing naturally out of the surrounding green woods, the pink-washed granite shape of the Sawmills, a thin column of smoke curling up from its main chimney.

We fell in love with the place on the spot, in due course bought it and spent five happy years there. Everything about the Old Sawmills was romantic and out of the ordinary. There was no road and you could only reach there by walking a mile along the river bank – or, preferably, by using one of the dinghies and inflatables we acquired. There was a quay at the main river end (where we were able periodically to keep *Sanu*), as well as a quay up by the house and our lives became very water orientated.

When we went shopping in Fowey we travelled down by Zodiac – when we went drinking on a Saturday night we used the same conveyance to cross to Polruan for an evening at the Russell Inn with our friends Jock and Edith. Ah, those were the days, weaving our way between yachts and motor cruisers and even large cargo boats, come to collect china clay. At the Sawmills itself there were several wooden chalets which various members of the family took over – upon weekends they would have friends over and many were the times when we all gathered on the quay, with the tide up, lighting a bonfire and singing songs or dancing to the Beatles and the Rolling Stones.

Seeing the Sawmills from afar everyone felt they were looking upon paradise, and in many ways so it was. However the fact is that hardly anyone has lived there for more than five years or so, and in due course the very isolation came to be a barrier to life – also, alas, the house was at the wrong end of Cornwall – and so in the end we took up our roots to put them back where they belong in West Cornwall. But – well, it was a once-in-a-lifetime experience the whole family remembers with great nostalgia.

P – is for ports. The sheer number we have visited! The other day I started counting and I haven't finished yet. We began nervously enough, like the tyros we were, with day excursions from Falmouth to far flung corners of the British Empire like Mevagissey (17 miles), Fowey (20 miles), Penzance (30 miles) – finally, greatly daring, over to the Scilly Isles, all of 60 miles. But then, gaining confidence, we set our horizons further a-sea. St Peter's Port, St Helier's, Cherbourg, Le Havre, Flushing, Veere, Wilhemstead, Rotterdam, Amsterdam, Borkum, Cuxhaven, Kiel Canal, Sonderborg, Svenberg, Copenhagen, Elsinore, Gothenberg, the Gota Canal, Stockholm, Visby, Bornholm ... later on the Brittany ports of Audierne, Concarneau, Belle Ile, Ile de Yeu, La Rochelle ... on and on, San Sebastian, Bilbao, Le Corunna, Vigo, Lexieos, Lisbon, Portimao, Gibraltar, Ceuta, Malaga, Almeira, Alicante, Ibiza, Palma, Port Vendres, Agde, Marseilles, the Golden Isles, St Tropez, Monte Carlo, Elba, Corsica, Sardinia, the Pontine Isles, the Aeolian Isles, Sicily, Malta, Greece and all its dreamed of islands, Hydra, Mykynos, Delos, Ios, Santorini, Siphnos, then the Dodecanese, Patmos, Leros, Kaliminos, Cos, Rhodes, followed by Crete (Aghios Nikolaos, Iraklion, Hania) and finally, the ultimate, Turkey – Bodrum, Marmaris, Feitye, Kas, Kekova ...

My head reels at the effort of remembering yet I have only named about a quarter of all the ports we backed *Sanu*'s fat bottom into. The total number I reckon would be around 250, many of them incredibly romantic in situation, like Symi in Greece where the local monks rang the monastery bell every time a boat arrived! Island ports were among our favourites, like Paxos in Greece, Ponza in Italy, Ibiza and Formentera in

Spain and Port Cros in France's Golden Isles. But if I had to make an arbitrary choice I would say our two favourite ports were one home and one away – Audierne on the coast of Brittany, and our own Newlyn here in the sheltered corner of Mount's Bay.

Q – is for queers, to use a slightly distasteful word – gay, I suppose, is a more pleasing version. Just as I have always hated any kind of racism, so I cannot bear the prejudices too often shown about sexual relationships (fortunately on the wane these days). What matters in life, surely, is the relationship – whether two people truly love one another, two friends are really friends. Some of my best friends are gay people of both sexes and often their set-ups, i.e. relationships with another of their own sex, are patently more rewarding and richer than all too many among our more 'normal' friends. I hope those of my readers who saw the recent BBC film 'Demelza's Baby', may agree with me that in this field we should live and let live, for happiness comes about in many strange ways. Besides (another reason for my having a soft spot for them) in my experience gay people are often truly gay in the old sense of the word, full of a sense of fun and joy of life, putting us old-fashioned normal creatures to shame.

R – is for rivers. Before I became caught up by the sea rivers were my great love. They always seem to me so romantic for one thing. When I was a boy I lived at East Molesey and most evenings delighted in riding on my bike along the leafy banks of the Thames, watching the motor cruisers gliding past Tagg's Island. Later on I hired a motor cruiser and we did a trip up the Thames from Thames Ditton to Goring and back – after that it was other rivers, the rivers on the Norfolk Broads, the River Shannon in Ireland – and of course the Rivers Fal and Fowey down here in Cornwall. Truly, river life is ever fascinating as we used to find at Fowey where at one moment the river was a deep racing small sea – then at low tide a place full of little island humps of exposed sand banks. You are constantly being surprised when travelling up rivers – as on the

River Fal where coming round a bend you encounter two or three gigantic cruise liners lying rustily at permanent moorings.

One of my most interesting experiences was travelling 250 miles up the River Seine into the heart of Paris. Like the sea, rivers have a life of their own.

S – can only be for *Sanu*, our dearly beloved old boat which I acquired with a legacy from my mother and owned for some twenty years before finally, owing to my ill health and Stephen's departure for several years to America, I felt unable to cope any longer and regretfully sold her. Like the Old Sawmills, *Sanu* was very much a once-in-a-lifetime experience. She was an Admiralty built MFV, the type of fishing boat to be seen in Newlyn – safe and sturdy, a fat old thing, but a boat that you knew would not let you down. Nor did she! In twenty years there were innumerable traumatic experiences – including two sinkings at the Scilly Isles and at Bilbao in Spain – but we survived them all. Both sinkings were by the land – out at sea, where the real dangers of possible death existed, *Sanu* never let us down. We never capsized, never were in the most desperate danger – somehow our valiant old warrior coped with everything the wild sea could throw at us (like waves thirty feet high, being caught in a cyclone, not to mention quite a few gales).

Sanu's exact measurements were 60 feet long by 18 feet wide by 7½ feet deep (14 feet to the top of the wheelhouse cabin) – a sizeable boat which allowed us to take many friends, as well as the family, on our voyages. And what voyages they were! We began very nervously sailing seventeen miles from Falmouth to Mevagissey – we ended up sailing 20,000 miles to such far flung corners of the world as Sweden in the North and Turkey in the South. Once we got *Sanu* out to the Mediterranean we kept her there for nearly ten years, and so we were able to really enjoy cruising, idly meandering from one Greek island to the next, or from one gay Italian port to another. How fortunate we were to be able to see so much of the western world from the deck of a boat of our own. There is no other experience in the world quite like it, especially arriving at some exotic new port after a long day's cruising of some wide stretch of sea.

For myself I found the navigation of perpetual interest, and prided myself that I alone was responsible for piloting us across all our 20,000 miles of voyaging, without ever seriously getting lost. (Once we were six miles out when bound for San Sebastian, after a 200 miles night crossing of part of the Bay of Biscay, but all we had to do was call out for directions to a passing Spanish fishing boat). Exploring new lands and places was part of the fascination of *Sanu*'s life – equally attractive was the social life aboard, the big evening meals sitting out on the stern under an awning with candles flickering – the daily six o'clock sundowners enjoyed from among our large stocks of incredibly cheap duty free drinks – the expeditions to sample the delights ashore of some attractive French bistro or a Greek taverna or perhaps one of those gaily casual Italian restaurants. And then back aboard *Sanu* we might all sit about the deck sniffing the fragrant night air and watching the riding anchor lights of other boats anchored around us.

Speaking of other boats reminds me of all the friends and new friends we made, on every trip – ah, the camaraderie of the sea. Bless you, dear old *Sanu*, for all the magic and wonder you brought into our lives.

T – is for travel – which really does broaden the mind. Thanks to *Sanu* we have done our fair share, but it has also pleased me that many members of our family have been off on their own account. Genevieve once went with a friend to India and hitched her way around, ending up at fabled Katmandu and brought back many wondrous tales. Stephen, so long a home bird, finally upped and travelled all the way across the Atlantic to sunny California where with his American wife Gina he lived some years at Santa Cruz – when he came back travel had indeed broadened his mind into many esoteric directions. As I get older I feel disinclined to do much travelling but I am always glad of all the opportunities I have had. Perhaps travel should be made a compulsory subject at all schools!

U – is for U-turns. Mrs Thatcher is fond of declaring she will never indulge in such a thing – but surely if we are wise we will admit that sometimes it is the answer to the more perplexing questions. I believe passionately in having principles and holding to them faithfully, but that does not mean that one should have opinions that may be wrong and cling to them blindly. In many spheres – not least in personal relationships for example – there may come a moment when change must be accepted if the day is to be saved. We all make mistakes – don't be afraid to admit your own.

I almost blush as I write these words for as a Scorpio I am one of the most hidebound of people, clinging to the rituals of life. Yet deep down I see the wisdom of the advice. Remember, it takes a person of stature to admit a mistake, to make the change. That old friend you have fallen out with – is the fault really all on the other side? That extreme political view you have clung to so doggedly – is it really the right one? That family feud, that business argument, and so on and so on – no, never be afraid to make a U-turn, my dear reader. You may be surprised at the new road to happiness you suddenly find yourself following.

V – is for Val – in this instance Stephen Val, my younger son by Jess, brother to Demelza and Genevieve. He is a Scorpio like myself, which has often led to our clashing – notably on the boat where each of us thought we knew best (and probably did!) – but underneath there is always the familiar bond of loving, I hope. As I imagine has been brought out in my autobiographical books Stephen has been a tower of strength in our family life, for he is tremendously practical and intelligent and has helped to solve many problems in the spheres of engineering and building and so forth – even earth removing! Stephen seems to have inherited many of my father's qualities, which means he is lively and dashing and very sociable. Musically he is very gifted indeed; without any lessons he made himself into a first class player on the piano and now has his own blues band in Penzance. He also composes and writes the lyrics of many lovely songs, often playing them to the accompaniment of a guitar (for some years he earned a respectable living as a busker in Paris).

Jess is particularly attached to Stephen because so often she is able to inspire him to bring to reality many of her wildest dreams – like the water-wheel or our famous patio. What I like about Stephen are some of his more vulnerable qualities – when he is down it often makes me want to weep and put an arm round his shoulder, it is my failing that I haven't done this enough. I once wrote a secret poem to Stephen, 'my shouting companion', in which I tried to assure him of the subterranean feelings that lie far below, – 'remember that beneath all the prickly branches love always lies waiting'.

Stephen is particularly a good companion to have at times of danger – I always remember an occasion on the boat when we were being tossed all over the place and everyone was very frightened – there was Stephen standing at the wheel and *singing* at the top of his voice! Devoted to his American wife Gina, and his son Paris and daughter Armira, Stephen is, like me, essentially the family man, giving himself up gratefully to all its many luxuries – not least being security.

W – is for writing – no, I don't mean the formation of scripts, I can hardly write my name legibly any more, thanks to the undermining influence of the typewriter. I mean, of course, that by which I live (and for which to a large extent I have lived). From the age of about eleven I had no doubts about what I wanted to be – I wanted to be a writer – and a writer I have been and enjoyed every minute of it. Of course, there is writing and writing, I can turn my hand to ordinary journalism or produce serious literature – each has its place, in my humble opinion.

I can honestly say that writing has never been a burden to me – to this day every morning of my life I go into my little office and take up a sheet of typing paper, put it into the typewriter and (sooner or later) begin typing. Sometimes there is the odd hang up but in general I have never found much difficulty in finding a subject. Autobiographies – well they often almost write themselves, it seems. Fiction presents more of a problem, and that is perhaps why in many ways I prefer writing fiction, it's more of a challenge.

Deep down I think of myself as essentially a short story writer, and would like to be remembered for such stories as 'The Clay Pool' or 'The Flame Swallower' or 'A Rose in Winter', or perhaps some of the longer novella-style stories, such as 'A Summer to Remember' or 'A Work of Art'. But then over the years I have become attached to some of the novels – in particular *Barbican's End* and *Rose*. I am really a very lucky man – for me writing has been both my occupation and my favourite hobby. To date I am 66 and have written 60 books, so I still hope to catch up and bring the figures level. Here's hoping!

X – is for the letter for which I cannot find a word. Let it remain that way, a reminder to us that in life there must always be something inexplicable. X marks the spot, X is the name of the secret benefactor, X hides the identity of so and so – yes, I am content to give X its freedom.

Y – is for youth. The older I get the more I admire the youth of today, or any other day for that matter. I always admired my own children in their younger days for the independence of spirit they showed. I still admire them, but am now beginning to notice my grandchildren as they grow up, and delight in seeing similar characteristics appearing. When I think of the sort of world we have created for our youth to inherit – well the mind boggles. I can only hope they will learn to forgive us our nuclear madnesses ... and that they never come to know the full horror of it all. Youth's a stuff that will endure runs an old saying – alas, as I know to my cost, that's not altogether true. But while it endures, during those magical years between the early teens and, say, thirty or so, the world belongs to the young, and rightly so. If they show less respect for their elders than they used to, who can blame them? All I ask of the youth today is that they are bold and brave and keep their eyes on some distant horizon. Long live our modern youth.

Z – must be for a comparatively late arrival into my life – Zambula, the Afro-rock band in which Demelza plays her congas. Down here in Cornwall, at least, they seem to have that something extra and have proved extremely popular. Every time Wendy the lead singer begins with her regular opening song, the plaintive 'Too Late', I sit back and know I am going to enjoy myself – the music is always lively and exciting, thanks largely to the conga playing of Demelza and Tito, the fuzzy-haired Ugandan member of the band (who also writes many of the chants and songs featured by the band). Zambula have an infectious way about their music – wherever they play it isn't long before people feel impelled to get up and start dancing to the music as it gets wilder and wilder. One day, I'm sure, Zambula will become nationally known rather than regionally – meantime, thanks for all the pleasure you've given to this aged fan.

VIII

Cornwall West and East

Whether it be east or west, Cornwall's fishing ports provide an endless source of interest. I never tire, for instance, of parking my car in some back street of Newlyn and then walking out along the north pier where sometimes there may be berthed over a hundred fishing boats of all shapes and sizes (sometimes their masts can be seen from quite a distance, like a forest). Everywhere the air is filled with the smell of tar and paint and diesel, and on most boats men in blue dungarees are bustling about either cleaning nets or preparing for a voyage, or maybe just unloading a catch brought in in rows of long plastic containers.

Newlyn is surely one of the most interesting ports not only in Cornwall but in Britain, for it has remained very much a working harbour and is in fact the most important commercial fishery in the South-West (more mackerel are brought into Newlyn than in any other port in the British Isles). And the harbour master once said jocularly – thinking wryly of St Ives which has, alas, given itself over to the holiday trade – 'here we lay nets for fish, not tourists'.

Nearly 200 boats operate from Newlyn, ranging from 90 foot trawlers equipped with Decca navigators, echo sounders, radio direction finders and telephones, down to one-man dories and dinghies, and the total annual value of fish landings is over the £1,000,000 mark. The types of fishing carried out are varied, ranging from trawling and long lining to shell fishing.

While Newlyn is a fascinating example of a large Cornish harbour (as are Mevagissey and Looe) some of the smaller ports are little gems, and everyone should visit traditional ports such as Porthleven or Coverack, or Port Isaac where boats are drawn up on the steep beach. In some of the smaller ports, like Polperro or Mousehole, in winter time great wooden bars are put across the harbour entrance to keep out the huge seas. This is a form of obstruction that was not always used with peaceful intent – in the past at both Fowey and Newlyn for instance chains used to be stretched across the harbour entrances, in the first instance to keep out pirates, and in the second to keep *in* irreligious Scots fishermen who dared to plan to go to sea on a Sunday.

It is at these smaller ports that old fishermen will still be found sitting on the harbour wall puffing their pipes, ready to spout their reminiscences about the good old days of seine netting and herring fishing and the like, now almost defunct. Seine netting, in particular, has quite a romantic history. At Sennen Cove where it is still carried out (though on a reduced scale) huge crowds would gather to watch the annual occasion when the vast seine net would be taken out to enclose a huge section of the inner bay (once a watcher or 'huer' had spotted the nearby shoals of mullet or pilchards). At a signal the net would be drawn in by dozens of willing hands until finally thousands of fish were dragged up on to the beach. When Jess and I lived at Peter's Cottage at Sennen Cove this was always a red letter day not to be missed for its atmosphere.

Thinking about Sennen Cove reminds me of a fascinating memoir of her childhood days there which Evelyn Scott Brown contributed to our *Cornish Review.* To this day, she remembered, whenever she smells a newly blown out candle, slightly acrid yet not unpleasant, she is immediately reminded of the tiny bedroom in the fisherman's cottage at Sennen Cove, where she was first taken for a holiday at the age of six. The cottage, solidly built by the fisherman's own hands, stood squarely facing the sea, its wall pebble-dashed with real beach pebbles, to keep out the weather. The front door had a central panel of rather garish coloured glass that appealed to her as a child, and Evelyn used to like to watch the sea through each gaudy colour in turn. She remembers the sudden stillness as that door was closed to shut out the unceasing roar of the sea and wind, and the endearing cosiness of the very homely cottage with its horsehair sofa and china dogs and – best of all – its enticing little bay window with seats.

She used to sit in this bay window watching the passers-by – in those days these were mainly fisherman, in blue jerseys and sea-boots, and one or two of them used to wave as they passed. Beyond, just the other side of the road, was the sea, in perpetual restless motion, and round to the right the magnificent sweeping curve of Whitesand Bay, bounded by Cape Cornwall and the Brison Rocks. It was a view she loved and she would lie happily in her little bed at night, till the monotonous surge of the waves pounding against the rocks finally lulled her to sleep. That incessant thunder was like music and somehow gave a sense of security, though of course those huge Atlantic breakers were in fact driven by a demonaic, almost sinister power, and were regarded with awe by the native population whose lives were one long battle with sea and storm.

The landlady of the cottage was a friendly soul with a squat, plump figure, very wrinkled brown skin and small dark eyes that lit up when she talked. She was a typical Cornishwoman, and had lived in Sennen all her life. Penzance was foreign soil to her, and when she went there she was always glad to get back to the familiar ground of Sennen. As a girl she had been very poor, and very hard-working. She told how she used to walk bare-footed along the cliffs to St Just, with a basket of fresh-caught fish that she hoped to sell there. Those hard days were over, but she still worked like a slave cooking and washing for all her visitors, in a hot, overcrowded kitchen with not even a sink.

That first holiday was one of many that the Scott Browns spent at Sennen Cove, mostly at Easter time, but occasionally at Christmas. Brought up to be a sturdy walker, with her parents, Evelyn explored all the enchanting cliff paths, and learned the way down to all the coves. It was hard to pick out a favourite, but she was especially fond of rugged Nanjizel, the first cove after Land's End; Nanjizel was utterly wild, with no habitation other than one house that was empty except for the summer of each year. The beach was of very white but coarse sand composed of broken-up sea-shells – later, after gales from a certain quarter, Nanjizel was bereft of sand, and was a formidable mass of rocks – a disappointment to a child.

Porthgwarra, the next cove, was most charming, and Evelyn remembered its granite cottages nestling against the cliff-side and its little pebbly beach and slipway and natural arch, the boats drawn up by an ancient windlass. On a sunny day, Porthgwarra was a delightfully warm spot, sheltered by the cliffs from the ever-blowing winds. At the back of the cove, behind some houses and gardens, a footpath wound up and along another stretch of cliff to St Levan and the long, narrow valley leading past the holy well and over a wooden plank bridge to Porthchapel. The steep descent was not easy but it was well worth while. The waves always seemed more powerful there than on any of the other beaches, and the child used to get an almost voluptuous thrill out of standing where the swiftly receding water dragged the sand violently from under her feet.

Down there, on the level, with the fierce, crashing breakers throwing up dazzling clouds of white spray that quickly drenched her face and made it tingle with brine she somehow felt weak and insignificant compared with the force of the elements. The sound of the sea was deafening, and to hear oneself speak at high tide it was necessary to retreat into one of the caves under the cliffs, from which refuge the splendid seascape could be surveyed at a safe distance. Porthchapel was lovely, yet terrifying, and after a while it was a relief to retrace steps up the valley past the gentle little stream.

Porthcurno, though a beautiful wide beach, always seemed a little formal compared with the smaller coves, and the houses of the Cable Station gave it a semi-Victorian look. They did not fit the landscape like the granite cottages of Porthgwarra. But further on lay the grand, rugged outline of Treryn Castle, a glorious pile of rock and the site of the elusive Logan stone. The next cove, Penberth, was another paradise, as was the lush valley that led to it from inland, when approached from Sennen Churchtown. The tiny brook with its bed of golden sand trickled its way through fields and woods, till it broadened out to a fair-sized stream, and the path led out to the lane that descended to the cove, past dream-houses with cool, well-watered gardens.

Sometimes the family would get as far as Lamorna, or the elusive St Loy, buried in woods, like a place on another planet. St Loy was a kind of lost Lyonesse of the mainland, so utterly remote did it seem. The aspect made it a place of almost tropical warmth, and they basked there in December in more comfort than some places would afford in June. In these days Lamorna was comparatively quiet and had few cars and no 'amenities'. The mile-long walk down the valley with the fine old trees and plashing stream, and the sudden, breathtaking vista of the tiny cove with its jetty and its handful of cottages – these lived long in the memory, just as the footpath to Mousehole, leading off steeply past the grey screes of the disused stone quarries, through snake-infested glades an area of natural marsh teeming with all kinds of bird-life, remained forever a vivid mental image of pure loveliness.

Going eastwards from Sennen, coves were fewer, and the cliff paths more narrow and precipitous. But they were very grand, and it was a delight to cross the sand and marram-grass at Vellandreath, and then clamber on till reaching the broad, smiling inlet of Nanquidno. The stream here typical of so many streams in the West Penwith valleys, rushed with careless impetuousness to fling itself into the sea. Although few of these streams had bridges or even good stepping-stones they were very much a feature of the district. Indeed the wide Nanquidno valley with its masses of gorse and blackthorn and rough-growing 'bents' seemed a vast no-mans-land, inhabited only by the cows which occasionally came to a bad end in the swamp and left their bones to rot as evidence of their misfortune.

Cape Cornwall, that symmetrical pyramid with the tall mineshaft on top, was a place very dear to the Scott Browns and they loved climbing up to the coastguard lookout, or crossing the 'saddle' at the back, to get a view of the further coastline towards Pendeen. The sea was always dashing against those jagged, black rocks, the gulls were always screaming, the cliffs were always gay with thrift and mesembrianthemum ... So, at a tender but impressionable age, a great love for West Penwith was born. Once born, it grew with each successive visit to Sennen, and in time young Evelyn came to know the cliff paths so well that she could find her own way anywhere – she even knew the lie of the rocky outcrops, that made so many of these paths potentially dangerous, just as she knew all the rather cumbersome Cornish stiles and the half-hidden short cuts through farms. The little peninsula, landmarked by the tall towers of Sennen and St Buryan churches, drew her irresistibly, as though it were some ancient home of her spirit. She loved the wilderness of it all, the untamed and untameable winds and waves and rocks. All these things gave her, in childhood, a strange blend of exhilaration and quiet contentment. Her world became temporarily narrowed down to the little world of West Penwith and 'it was always a jolt to leave that world for the other, everyday world of home'.

I was always rather proud of the high standard we seemed to achieve in the *Cornish Review* in our evocative pieces about various Cornish beauty spots. There are dozens to which I could legitimately draw attention – in an earlier book, for example, I quoted from a marvellously alive account of a walk around Land's End by M.A. Hollingham. That was full of fascinating information about the terrain – similarly there is much absorbing detail in this kind in an article Michael Williams once wrote for us after riding on horseback across Bodmin Moor, one of Cornwall's greatest (and most mysterious) attractions. Take a look, he said, at the ordnance survey map:

'Twelve Men's Moor, so called because of the twelve tenants of Launceston Priory which owned Bodmin Manor in the 13th century, Temple, where the Templars incredibly built a Norman church, in which couples were married without banns, Stripple Stones, below Hawk's Tor, a Bronze Age momument stretching 180 feet, the Cheeswring, a colony of fantastic rocks and King Doniert's Throne – the very names quicken the imagination. Lord's Waste, Black Rock, Draynes, Maiden Tor and Hard Head – places read like extracts from a novel.

'St Neot, standing at the southern edge, is a story of its own. The stained glass windows of the parish church are fit for any cathedral. "Who can look at them," asked Charles Causley, "and doubt Cornwall's creative talent?" Legends thickly surround St Neot himself. Some believe he was an elder brother of Alfred, that he was the first head of Oxford University, that he performed miracles and that he was a dwarf and spent hours, each day, immersed to the neck in his well – and in meditation.

'Once the Moor – or to be precise St Breward, formerly Simonsward – was the most thickly populated area in Cornwall. 3,000 years before the stable birth at Bethlehem, ancient man encamped here. A thousand years later the Bronze Age people, a more sophisticated race, arrived; King Arthur's so-called Hall, a rectangular enclosure, is thought to belong to this era. Then came the Celts, from whom we Cornish are descended. The Celts, with their knowledge of the wheel which they employed for ploughing, were the pioneer farmers. Fields and place names are reminders of their contribution. Tin was mined on the Moor. Rakes remain – huge furrows in the ground made by miners – but the noise of labour died long ago. De Lank Quarry, though, flourishes.

'Cathedral of the Moor is the church of St Nonna's at Altarnun – the biggest parish in the county: 15,000 acres. The village itself is little more than a street of aged cottages, surrounded by elms and beeches, but the eyes automatically go to St Nonna's 130 foot tower, the tallest of all Cornish churches, it took more than a generation to construct. The stone, that built this church, came from three sources: from unquarried stone, lying on the moor, from the previous Norman church and from the Mansion of the Trelawney Family who in the 15th century moved to Trelawne. St Nonna's gems are 79 beautifully carved bench ends. They date from 1510 to 1530 and are carved with the Instruments of the Passion, a man with a cauldron, another with bagpipes, a fiddler – a mixture of parish worthies, common sights, renaissance designs and religious themes. The bench end next to the font gives the name of the carver as Robert Daye. Is he only a name? Do we know nothing of this Cornish craftsman?

'The old Methodist Meeting House is but a cricketer's throw from the churchyard gate. John Wesley's head, carved by Nevil Northley Burnard at the age of 16, is above the door: eyes toward Five Lanes. Burnard was born at Altarnun three years after Waterloo; the son of a stone mason, he went to London and, like Opie, won fame but died penniless and forgotten in Redruth Workhouse. Only in 1954 – 76 years after his death – was he given a headstone in Camborne graveyard. His bones really should be under the soil of this churchyard at Altarnun, where there are two headstones he carved at the age of 14. One on the west of Isbell's Tomb is presumably that of his grandfather and grandmother; this slate carries an eagle flying into rays of sunlight and the second, positioned near the Vicarage garden gate, concerns a young cousin and bears the Angel of the Last Trump – Burnard's very first effort. The boy's tools were nails, sharpened on a grinding stone.

'Services have always been unusual at St Nonna in that the priest has celebrated Holy Eucharist from the east side of the

High Altar, facing his flock – as does the Pope. There have been close links here too between Methodists and Anglicans. Samuel Hart, a former vicar, observed in 1821: "There are no Papists in the parish, but many Wesleyan Methodists who for the most part frequent the church." Separation at Altarnun came slowly, reluctantly.

'The holy well at Altarnun was reputed to have healing powers over the insane. Richard Carew, in his *Survey of Cornwall*, described the practice of plunging a frantic person in the water and then conveying him to the church where masses were said. "If his wits returned, St Nun had the thanks, but if there appeared some small amendment, he was bowseened again and again, while there remained in him any hope of life or recovery."

'Long ago ponies, laden with contraband from Boscastle, travelled inland to secret rendezvous. Some, under night's black coat, almost certainly used the roads around Altarnun; Baring-Gould, author of "Onward Christian Soldiers" and famous ferreter of Cornish history and legends, found a house nearby containing a chamber, hidden at the back of a hearth – a nook for smuggled spirits and tobacco.

'Over at Five Lanes a present-day traveller meets the grey ribbon of the A30. Left the road climbs to the Cornish gateway, Launceston, eight and a half miles away. Right the road leads on to the county town of Bodmin. In the late eighteenth and nineteenth centuries the main artery of Cornwall ran through Launceston, across the Moor and down to Truro. Stage and mail coaches moved through this "howling wilderness". Today cars, buses and lorries eat up the miles and grazing animals live dangerously. Mary Yelland, peering out of the coach window in the opening chapter of Daphne du Maurier's best-seller, *Jamaica Inn*, set a century and a half ago, saw " … mile upon mile of bleak moorland, dark and untraversed, rolling like a desert land to some unseen horizon." The Moor, in fact, stretches twelve miles north to south and eleven miles east to west. In the south a few minor roads are tributaries of the A38. Northward, roads grow scarce and tracks disappear.'

'F.E. Baines, reminiscing in 1895, referred to two moorland inns:

' "The King's Head at Five Lanes stands as of yore – a solid, square-set building, unchanged by sixty years of restful ease. Jamaica Inn, now a temperance house, was built by a retired Jamaica settler. Because of its erection at a spot where the great road traverses a desolate moor, the good folk of Altarnun, close by, said it was a "bould venture". In course of time a village sprang up around the inn, and a "bould venture" gave place to a good Cornish name of Bolventor. Should anyone assail the solid foundations of this story, I might triumphantly retort that on Stockdales' careful map of 1824 there is to be found Jamaica Inn, but not Bolventor, and that on the new ordnance map of 1889 will be found Bolventor, but no Jamaica Inn.' "

'The King's Head had links with the Civil War. Cromwell is reputed to have been routed in this area but managed to escape with all the food and wines, compelling Royalists to spend a night on their empty bellies! Sir Richard Grenville is also associated with the inn and Peggy Bray, a former owner, is said to take an occasional ghostly stroll.

'Jamaica Inn, thanks to Dame Daphne du Maurier's pen, is one of the best known inns in England. Many Americans count it as a 'must' on their tours to the South-West. It is a dour, slated Georgian building. Some dislike its commercialization – there is a gift shop section and bars are named after characters in the story – but, for others, the stone-flagged floors, oak beams, granite fireplaces, with their smouldering logs, the cobbled yard and creaking smuggler's sign all combine in generating an aura of the past. At the height of the holiday season pints and pasties disappear by the thousand.'

Just over a mile away on a byroad that leads to St Neot lies Dozmary Pool, a saucer-like depression to the south-west of

Fowey Valley, a mile in circumference and 500 yards across. There was a theory that the pool was bottomless, but in 1869 it dried up and drowned the notion. This sheet of water is where Sir Bedivere, in reluctant obedience to the dying King Arthur, traditionally threw away the sword Excalibur. Some literary scholars, however, consider Loe Pool, near Helston, as the more likely situation. One guidebook I recently read suggested that Arthurian legend apart, Dozmary was unworthy of visiting. C.E. Vulliamy, in *Unknown Cornwall*, thought differently;

' ... nowhere on earth,' he wrote, 'are there landscapes more austerely beautiful, more wonderful in their changes of mood and colour, or more splendid in outline ... The Pool in its placid moods, when it becomes a mirror reflecting the forms of moor and cloud, has a charm so powerful, yet so elusive, that it can only be conveyed to you in pictures: the limits of descriptive writing are soon reached when we are dealing with the sublimely simple in landscape and the charm of Dozmary is composed visually of the simplest elements – water, sky and earth. Indeed the value of much of the Cornish landscape is essentially a pictorial value, a value of breadth and space, of sky and cloud, of wide surfaces and large, simple forms. The landscapes of literature are otherwise: crowded with detail or incident or movement, like the canvases of Lorrain.'

Another Dozmary legend concerns John Tregeagle, an unjust steward. He was charged – by the spirits – for his misdeeds and was sentenced to bail out Dozmary with a leaky limpet-shell. Tregeagle was so tormented by the impossibility of his task that he fled to Roche Rock, where hammering and howling on the door of the chapel, he begged the saints to let him in. Children of past generations were told that the storm noises were Tregeagle and his hell hounds hunting on the Moor, and even today the expression 'howling like a Tregeagle' remains part of a Cornishman's vocabulary.

Where do you end on Bodmin Moor? There is no obvious,

really final full-stop. As Thomas Burke wrote of Tintagel:

' ... there is little one can say ... Description conveys nothing, and reflections are meaningless. What it has to give must be received individually ... '

The same is true of this weird, wild world.

IX

The Sea is Always There

The sea *is* Cornwall, to a large degree – like a lover it constantly caresses and embraces every nook and cranny of the strange mass of land which hurls itself out in granite abandon into the face of three oceans – the English Channel in the south, the Atlantic Ocean in the west, and the Irish Sea and the Bristol Channel in the north. Just as it is no doubt impossible to understand the true meaning of Scotland without considering the place in its life and history of those magnificent peaked Highlands, so the stranger to Cornwall, though he must indeed understand as the poet said that 'the bones of this land are not speechless', above all, has to grasp the true significance of the greeny blue waters forever lapping at the sandy edges of England's longest and most romantic stretch of coastline.

When I once wrote that it would be difficult to think of a place like Cornwall on the same level as Essex or Surrey, Kent or Berkshire, or Northamptonshire, I was thinking of the sea as well as the land. Many counties, of course, are cut off completely from the sea, but among those that have a coastline like Kent and Sussex, the contrast with somewhere like Cornwall can sometimes be a stunning one. I have lived in both Kent and Sussex, and of course both these counties have their share of savage seas and storms, and equally of placid sunny days and children playing on the sands; but if only in their basic flatness their relationship with the sea seems to lack something of the mystery and grandeur immediately visible in almost any part of Cornwall. Even in its colouring, the sea seems different – certainly around the South Eastern Coast, the sea often seems grey and uninteresting, whereas along the Cornish coast the dancing waves are literally coloured an exotic mixture of green and blue, flecked sometimes with silver.

Near to my home at Tresidder we have some of the loveliest coves in Cornwall – Penberth, Porthgwarra, Nanijizel, St Levan. Here the waters are absolutely translucent, the sands bleached a perfect white; it could be somewhere on the Continent, in the Mediterranean, were it not for the restless surging tide, with a rise and fall of twenty feet or so. Down almost every cliff face there are winding steps which take you down into a magical world of caves and rock pools – many of them in coves that are cut off when the tide is in, their treasures available for only an hour or two.

It is in areas like this, and over at Botallack and Gurnard's Head on the North Coast, that the intrepid visitor can take advantage of one of the subtle combinations of sea and land; rock climbing. Here is an attempt by a friend of mine, climber Mike Borg Banks, to capture the feeling of such an experience:

'Because the tide was low we were able to get right down to the very bottom of the climb at the base of the cliffs. Although the surface of the sea was smooth on this sunny, windless day, great long oily rollers were sweeping in. They pounded themselves into surf on the sands by Logan Rock and thundered against the outcrop of rocks on which we were standing. The granite that we were to climb rose sheer above for some two hundred and fifty feet before its tooth-like summit made a cruel silhouette against a metallic sky. We uncoiled our nylon climbing rope, each taking an end tied a bowline around our waist. I was all too well aware that this climb was of a "severe" standard, and would tax both nerve and strength before the top were attained.

'As I approached the first pitch of the climb I felt again that cold pang that I have come to know so well, almost to expect at this stage. In the presence of such an ageless and immutable massif, I experience a deep feeling of inferiority and impotence, as if it were an impertinence to sully those dignified granite walls with climbing boots and festoon them with ropes. But the feeling is transient in the face of the reality of the rock. The eyes and spirit were torn down from the soaring heights to the very material problem of negotiating the first pitch. This was in the form of a crack in the cliff wall sufficiently wide to admit a man's body, and is described in mountaineering jargon as a chimney. I squeezed into this tomblike cavity, made chilly by the morning tide. The granite here was washed hard and smooth by the ceaseless action of the sea, and consequently presented an utter lack of holds. It was a worthy start to a worthy climb, and had to be ascended in the manner traditional to chimneys. A concerted heave, groan, grab and grunt gains a few precious inches, which must at all costs be retained by jamming the knees or elbows until another effort carries the climber yet a few inches more. I painfully ascended the cold clammy walls until, panting and weary, I emerged on to a sunny ledge; all apathy and apprehension had now vanished.

'The granite, being well above the high-water mark, had changed from the cold, slippery texture of the chimney to that rough, fawn rock, mottled with lichen, which besides being a delight to the eye afforded a host of small but safe footholds to the jagged teeth of the tricouni climbing nails set around the edges of our climbing boots. Here the cliffs rose above, lying just a few degrees back from the vertical. A rough, broken line of weakness on the left indicated the only reasonable route. I climbed out round an awkward ascending corner which, although plentifully supplied with holds, tended to throw the climber off balance to the left. Above, the cliffs rose again sheer, the holds being ample for toes and fingers. Careful movements and good technique triumphed, until once again I tied myself to the rock. I was now striking form, and the rough granite cliff unrolled in front of me like a dappled carpet.

'It was the mood that makes one relish difficulties, so that the granite that looked so forbidding from below, now appeared to be smiling and encouraging me. I suddenly became conscious that the noise of the surf had mellowed and a gentle breeze was fanning my cheek. Only then was I aware that I had ascended about a hundred and fifty feet, the rollers creaming far below ... '

The climber has an unusual, even an extraordinary experience of the sea, suspended as he is between it and the land. Another fascinating way of experiencing the sea in Cornwall is from a boat. For many years we have enjoyed voyaging in our old motor fishing vessel *Sanu* around the coast of Cornwall. To this day I have never forgotten our first arrival, when we had bought our boat 'up country' at Southampton and how, after passing the striking Eddystone Lighthouse, a lonely finger of granite sticking out of the sea, forty miles out from Plymouth, at last with an accompanying blaze of mid-day sunshine we emerged from a sea mist – and there was Cornwall spread out in a vast jewelled sweep all around: Looe, Polperro, Fowey, St Austell Bay, the dreaded Dodman Head, Portscatho, St Anthony Head with its black and white lighthouse and the opposite hump of Pendennis Castle, Helford and the vague outline of the Manacles – on the horizon the tall white building of the famous Lizard Lighthouse. It was all wild and beautiful.

Later, we were to pass the rugged cliffs around Lamorna Cove and Penberth, Land's End and then Cape Cornwall, steering well clear of the Brisons, then taking a bearing on Pendeen Lighthouse and Botallack's crumbling minestacks as we headed eastwards up the north Cornish coast past the lovely cliffs of Gurnard's Head and Zennor, across St Ives Bay, on and on up the wild coast so bereft of shelter save for Hayle and Padstow, both with their awkward sand-bars. On past Trebetherick and Polzeath, Portquin and Port Isaac, Boscastle and Tintagel:

Whence men might see wide east and west in one
And on one sea waned moon and mounting sun.

And severed from the sea rock's base, where stand
Some worn walls yet, they saw the broken strand,
The beachless cliff that in the sheer sea dips,
The sleepless shore inexorable to ships,
And the straight causeway's bare gaunt spine between
The sea-spanned walls and naked mainland's green.

as it was once put by Algernon Swinburne, one of the dozens of great poets who have been inspired to write about the Cornish coastline.

The best way to approach Cornwall is from the sea, sailing from Southern Ireland to the Hayle estuary as the first traders did more than 2000 years ago. Daphne du Maurier once said this and she imagined arriving with the same shock of surprise and relief. After a stormy passage with the prevailing sou'westerly wind veering between the quarter and hard astern, one would encounter the inhospitable rock-bound Cornish claw thrusting into the Atlantic in quest of victims to find the immediate north west of its scaley hump, a welcome haven. Then, as today, the contrast was profound between the forbidding grandeur of the coastline about Land's End, with its hinterland of granite tors, and the sudden emergence of St Ives Bay, an encircling arm protecting the shallows and the yellow sands and the estuary of Hayle.

'For the watcher today, crouching among the sand dunes and the tufted grass, looking seaward to where the shallows run, imagination can take a riotous course, picturing line upon line of high-powered flat bottomed craft, brightly coloured, their sails abeam, entering the river with the flood tide. What cries and oaths, what turbulence of Mediterranean chatter interspersed with Irish, as the traders ran their vessels on the sand or anchored them to swing midstream, what speedy loading or unloading of cargo between ship and settlement. What feasting, when the work was done, beside a fire of turf and furze; what interchange of views with dance and conquest! And then the image fades and the dreamer, stiff from crouching in the dunes, sees how the sand has, through the centuries, invaded the coastal countryside north of Hayle. Hurricanes, in the long distant past, whipped up the swirling mass into dense clouds which settled on the land below. Whole farmsteads were overwhelmed and now lie buried, while the waste land known as the towans, a mixture of sand and searush – a stiff stemmed reedy grass planted in the old days by the inhabitants to stay the driving sand – stretches through Phillack and Gwithian parishes until the ground rises into the headland of Godrevy Point. Gales and storms have been ever frequent on both north and south Cornish coasts, bringing havoc and disaster with them and a multitude of wrecks, but a hurricane of sand, destroying homes, was the grim fate of these Gwithian farmers.'*

This vivid picture of just a small section of the Cornish coastline comes from the pen of a writer who in her time, together with her husband the late General Sir Frederick Browning, spent a great deal of time sailing in Cornish waters. If you live in Cornwall then it is more than likely that sooner or later the sea will draw you into its world, either sailing or swimming, or perhaps indulging in the almost exclusively Cornish sport of surfing.

I have done all these things: when our family was young we lived in a house facing the great Atlantic rollers on Porthmeor Beach at St Ives, and the great delight each day was for all of us, carrying our slender surf boards, to march out until the sea was up to our necks; then turning and waiting for the right wave, suddenly thrusting the board forward, launching ourselves as into space, kicking wildly with our feet, hoping to be caught up in the relentless momentum of the wave, and carried on in a marvellous flurry of sound and speed until eventually we would be washed up, glowing with exhilaration, on the white sandy beach. Surfing is a sport almost unique, in the British Isles, to Cornwall: there are some excellent surfing

* *Vanishing Cornwall* by Daphne du Maurier. Reproduced by permission of Curtis Brown Ltd on behalf of Daphne du Maurier. Copyright Daphne du Maurier 1967.

beaches all along the North Coast notably at Newquay, Perranporth, Polzeath and Bude.

Later on, when we had our own boat we were able to explore the Cornish sea in more detail, venturing into hidden coves and crannies, down great estuaries like the Fal and Fowey, entering busy fishing ports such as Mevagissey and Newlyn, teaming with the fishing folk's life – or across the great Atlantic swell to the magical, mystical humps of the Isles of Scilly.

The sea is such an integral, all important part of Cornwall that it is often literally impossible to separate the two things, to say where one begins and the other ends. Of course, technically the sea ends where the tide leaves its wriggling line of sea shells and seaweed and strange ridges of sand (which on many huge beaches, like Whitesand Bay, Sennen, change formation every day) – but in fact the *influence* of the sea carries on far beyond the tide line, permeating not merely the immediate surroundings but, I would say, the entire atmosphere of the whole of Cornwall. After all, not only does Cornwall possess the longest coastline in the British Isles, there is also the extremely relevant factor that almost nowhere in the strange, elongated county can you be more than a dozen or so miles from if not the sea, then some estuary or river. Small wonder that, along with their well known propensity for being found tunnelling into the earth down mines all over the world, the other most likely occupation of the Cornish is to be sailing the seven seas. After all, in such a grandiose sea-enclosed world, it is only doing what comes naturally.

First, though, in any consideration of the sea in Cornwall's life, or for that matter Cornwall in the sea's life (for as I say the two are interwoven like perpetual lovers) I think one simply must consider the sheer physical majesty of the ever-changing seascape. It is little wonder that this sort of scenery has drawn some of the finest painters of our time: there are records of several visits to Cornwall in the early part of the nineteenth century of the great J.M.W. Turner, including one journey of hundreds of miles during which he made many sketches. He followed the inevitable southern coastal route, Looe, Fowey, Falmouth, Lizard, Penzance and Mount's Bay, and then up the North Coast via St Ives, Newquay, Padstow, Tintagel, Boscastle, Bude. Some of his paintings were comparatively conventional – pictures like 'St Mawes at the Pilchard Season' now in the Tate Gallery, and 'Saltash with the Water Ferry' owned by the Metropolitan Museum, New York. But it was when he came to the truly dramatic and romantic spots on the Cornish coast that the sparks, or rather the paint began to fly. When he produced his painting 'Longships Lighthouse Land's End', it was described by John Ruskin as a picture full of the energy of storm, fiery in haste, and yet flinging back out of its motion the fitful swirls of bounding drift, of tortured vapour tossed up like man's hands, as in defiance of the tempest' ... waves defeated by walls of rock and beaten back until the whole surface of the sea becomes one dizzy whirl of rushing, writhing, tortured undirected rage, bounding and crashing and coiling in an anarchy of enormous power'.

There is another engraving by Turner entitled 'The Lost Sailor' or 'Storm over the Lizard' showing again an immense wave about to engulf the world. Through films of spray looms a towering cliff; in the distance a rocky headland is surmounted by a small building, probably one of the original Lizard lighthouses; and there is a pathetic glimpse of a body of a lost sailor being tossed like flotsam among wreckage in the dip of terrifying waves.

Some critics accused Turner of painting Cornwall larger than life, increasing the menace of the huge waves, the steepness of cliffs, even the size of the enchanting fairybook St Michael's Mount, but in truth he was only responding, as every creative artist has done, to the ultimate melodrama of the wild coastline.

It is hardly surprising that rough seas, spray-covered cliffs and above all horrendous shipwrecks loom large in the sea mythology of Cornwall. Today more than ever there is quite a literature of books devoted to the history of Cornish shipwrecks, and fascinating reading they are (especially those of the local historian Cyril Noall). Yet often, to be truthful, everything contained in these detailed accounts may well be summed up more vividly, more unforgettably, in a single photograph as, for instance, in the marvellous photographs of the Gibson family of St Mary's Isles of Scilly, generations of whom carried on the family tradition of photographing major wrecks in that storm-bound area. Not long ago the eminent author John Fowles edited and introduced a remarkable collection of these photographs but even he, craftsman though he is in words, gave the impression of feeling that there was little he could add to the stark impact of those terrifying photographs of lovely old barquentines and majestic three-masted schooners being pounded to pieces by the merciless sea.

Of course the sea is not always in such angry moods, and Cornwall can provide a smiling face, like any other warring tiger! Though the county has few rivers, those that exist are fascinating ones to explore, particularly the Fal, which provides at its Falmouth entrance what is regarded as one of the world's finest natural harbours, and where the narrowing river, winding its way up to the county's capital town of Truro, is full of interest to the naturalist and bird lover, with winding bends overhung by trees (an unfamiliar sight in a land generally scoured clean of trees by relentless winds). I have often chugged up the Fal, though I have done this more often on its neighbour eastwards, the River Fowey, where we lived five years at an old mill near Golant, about three miles up river. Here all is calm and peaceful, the tide ebbs and flows, dozens of gaily painted boats bob at their moorings, and as our near neighbour, Daphne du Maurier once observed,* birds are everywhere:

'Oyster-catchers – "sea-pie" to the Cornish – with a quick seeping cry swoop to the mudbanks in a flash of black and white. The smaller redshank and sanderling scurry to probe

* *Vanishing Cornwall*, op. cit.

the slate. Further up river, where a dead branch of a fallen tree, strung about with seaweed, overhangs the water, a heron stalks, prinking his way like some grave professor fearing to lose a galosh, then suddenly stands and broods, his wings humped, his head buried in his feathers. Later the tide slackens the trees darken, the birds are hushed, and there is no sound except the whisper of water past the anchor chain until, if the yachtsman is lucky, he will hear, during the magic moments before true dusk falls, the night-jar call. It is a summons unlike any other, churring, low, strangely compelling, so that on first hearing it you must think of neither bird nor beast but of some forgotten species, scaly lizard cross-bred with a toad. There is no sweetness here, no nightingale passion, no owl foreboding; the call is primitive, insistent, with a rhythmic rise and fall, coming not from the wooded slopes but from open ground beyond, where amidst foxglove and gorse the night-jar crouches.'

The silent reaches of the Fowey and Fal rivers, and of the Camel on the north coast, are the very opposite to the wild seas of the rocky coastline. Somewhere in between the two extremes stand the long white sandy beaches with which Cornwall abounds – for, as with everything in Cornwall, many of these beaches are often not all that they seem. Thus at Harlyn, on the north coast, an ancient burial ground was discovered when, fifteen feet below the surface, a slate coffin was found containing a human skeleton. Removal of some 2,000 tons of sand disclosed about 150 such burials. Many of the skeletons were in a good state of preservation, buried in a crouched position, heads pointing to magnetic north. Tools were found, including stone spindle whorls for spinning and querns for grinding corn, and there were traces of fire and charcoal and shells. A house and a museum have now been built and can be visited. Archaeologists are now inclined to think that the burials go back as far as 7000 years. Certainly there is a strange atmosphere at Harlyn Bay, especially coming from the sandy beach into the little museum. Jack Clemo, the Cornish poet, captured it thus:

We question together, our feet still tingling
From the Atlantic swirl on shingle cleared of graves.
What deities were worshipped
Inside the delicate white curve
Of that girl's skull? Did she tramp inland,
Perform weird rites on the knoll
We call Brown Willy, her dark breasts stripped
In frenzy at full moon?

At Gwithian, further west along the north coast, there is a popular legend of a whole village buried under the sands, 'lost land of Langarrow sleeping under silent sandy waves', and this legend crops up elsewhere around the Cornish coastline. But the beaches have other surprises, too. At Porthcurno, for instance, one of the finest beaches in the whole of Cornwall, the visitor has three surprises in store. First, he will find himself standing on the very sands under which the huge telephone cables run from the nearby Cable and Wireless headquarters down into the sea and way across the Atlantic to America.

Second, over to the west he can see one of the most famous clifftops in Cornwall, the Logan Rock, a huge rock balanced like an upraised finger which was supposed once to have been toppled over for a bet by a naval lieutenant – his employers, the Royal Navy, forced him at his own expense to have the rock put back! Third, and by no means last, a short climb up some cliff steps will bring the visitor to the wonder of the Minack Theatre, about which I have written before. Hewn out of the rocks, it looks far out over the waters of Mount's Bay to the distant winking light of the Lizard Lighthouse.

Lighthouses, of course, have played an important part in the history of Cornwall and the sea. Cornwall has the largest quota of major lighthouses in Britain, and of course some of the most famous – including the Lizard and Land's End, and Bishop Rock, on the Scillies. I suppose pre-eminent among all the eleven major lighthouses is the Lizard, whose familiar three second flash has so often been recognised with relief by ships that have battled their way across the usually turbulent Bay of Biscay and into the English Channel. The late Sir Francis Chichester, for instance, was one of dozens of long distance yachtsmen for whom the friendly Lizard was a first welcome home signal.

The Lizard is in fact the oldest lighthouse in Britain, let alone Cornwall. It began when Sir John Killigrew, head of one of Cornwall's oldest and most renowned families, the Killigrews of Falmouth, obtained a patent from James I to erect a lighthouse at a cost of some £500. He hoped – vainly as it happened – to maintain the light by means of voluntary contributions from owners of ships which benefited from the service, which finally began in the year 1619. The benefits were made full use of but the contributions were practically non-existent and in the end that particular 'light that never failed' was extinguished as an economic necessity. However about a century later, Thomas Fonnerau built a four tower lighthouse with coal-burning lights at the Lizard and this operated well into the nineteenth century. The present elongated structure was then set up and has remained ever since dominating a large area of the south western coast of England.

Although the lighthouse has retained much the same appearance for so long, there have been marked changes on the technological side. Today the lighthouse is fully electric with the most powerful beam in the British Isles – no less than 4,000,000 candlepower! This and the fact that the lighthouse is 250 feet above the sea level enables the beam to cover an effective distance of nearly 22 miles – a fact we have appreciated on more than one occasion when returning on our old MFV *Sanu* from some cross-Channel excursion – though not on the very first occasion when being very tired I became mesmerised with the light and sailed dangerously close, developing hallucinations that I could see people moving around on the shore *in the dark*! Fortunately I had the sense in the end to turn out seawards before we impaled ourselves on one of those awful jagged rocks that poke out of the sea in front of Lizard Point.

Cornwall's other oldest lighthouse is at the other extreme from the Lizard in more senses than one – at Pendeen on the grim northern coast, close by a dark and ugly mining village. Although the inland district is dull, the coastline itself is extremely beautiful, stretching from Cape Cornwall to Gurnard's Head and Zennor and St Ives. And then, just across St Ives Bay one comes to the next lighthouse in line, Godrevy, whose winking light I used to see every night for nearly ten years during the time we lived at St Ives. Like so many outlying rock or island lighthouses Godrevy was put up after a particularly disastrous shipwreck on the villainous Stones, a reef stretching across part of St Ives Bay. (Virginia Woolf enhanced the fame of Godrevy in her novel *To the Lighthouse*).

During a recent tour I took the opportunity to visit two more of the four lighthouses which are open to the public – Trevose Head, near Padstow, and the spectacularly situated St Anthony Head lighthouse at the entrance of one of England's great natural harbours at Falmouth. I shall always remember standing on that low headland beside St Anthony looking across to Pendennis Castle on the opposite side and in between seeing the white sails of yachts of all sizes and shapes, as well as the mountainous steel silhouettes of cargo ships bound for the docks at Falmouth. Nearer to home, there is the Longships, set on the Carn Brea rocks about a mile west of Land's End itself – a lighthouse so near to the land that the keepers and their wives can semaphore to each other! The wives live in a row of white coastguard houses on the cliffs at Sennen – yet because of the expanse of extremely dangerous waters they might as well be a hundred miles away as far as actual contact is concerned.

I expect quite a few readers have leaned on a wall or rock at Land's End and stared out in wonder at the lonely lighthouse. If you have been lucky enough to have done so on a day of Atlantic gales you will surely have marvelled at the sight – a not infrequent one by any means – of huge waves whose spray reaches up to the window panes of the light lanterns, nearly 120 feet high. Altogether the Longships presents quite an eerie picture and not surprisingly there are many hair-raising stories about keepers going mad and drowning and so forth. Some of the most vivid accounts of the atmosphere are captured in a favourite old book of mine, which you can still find in second-hand bookshops, *Watchers on the Longships* by James F. Cobb.

Another extremely functional Cornish lighthouse is the Wolf, but this is something very much out of the ordinary for, like the Eddystone off Plymouth, it is set far out to sea. I have often sailed close by and would estimate the Wolf rock to be about ten miles from the mainland. The lighthouse is an imposing and ingenious edifice, a 135 foot tower painstakingly built up with dove-tailed granite blocks on top of rock formations at a total cost of £62,726. Being so far out to sea, the Wolf light is a great boon to sailors who can take cross-bearings with it as is the Longships and the Lizard and, for that matter, the two main lighthouses on the Isles of Scilly: the famous Bishop, and Round Island, on the north-west side.

The Bishop's designer, James Walker, based its structure on the ideas of Smeaton's Eddystone, a series of two ton granite blocks set into pre-selected positions. Remembering that every piece of granite had to be shipped from the mainland and hauled into position, often in the face of the most inclement weather, it is little wonder that the whole project took seven years. The total costs of the Bishop are said to have exceeded £100,000 but all these expensive precautions are very necessary – records show that during one storm waves were so high that they tore a 5 cwt foghorn out of its fastenings! As readers of the national newspapers may remember, keepers on the Bishop have been marooned there by bad weather. Recently plans were in hand to build helicopter platforms on both Bishop and Round Island.

In all this consideration of the savage sea in Cornwall I find I am mesmerised by the restless sea itself, as if it were a living thing, enveloping us endlessly in its constantly moving world. Of course this is true – yet there is another aspect of the sea-life of Cornwall which is worth mentioning, as it remains one of the most delightful of all pleasures which the proximity of great oceans has given to this strange land. I am thinking now of the boisterous, lively, crowded, bustling harbour-life to be found all along the coast of Cornwall, from busy fishing ports like Looe and its smaller companion, Polperro, in the south-east corner, through Fowey and Mevagissey and small Lizard ports like Coverack and Cadgwith and Porthleven, down to the big Mount's Bay port of Newlyn on the south west. On the more inhospitable north coast of Cornwall the fishing ports are fewer and further between, but there are some marvellous miniature ones, like Port Isaac and Boscastle, as well as sizeable ports at St Ives and Padstow. Whether it be north or south, the Cornish fishing ports provide an endless source of interest.

The sea and Cornwall, Cornwall and the sea – the permutations are endless for there is as much variety to be dredged out of one subject as the other. What about smuggling, that favourite pastime – once indeed practically a major industry – of Cornwall not so long ago? Cornwall is by no means the only English coastal county to have known the smuggling trade, but it is certainly one of the very busiest centres of what used to be known, euphemistically, as 'Free Trade'.

It is important to remember that in olden days the smuggler was perhaps the most popular law-breaker there has ever been – a kind of Robin Hood of the coast, who cheated the Government to bring luxuries within the reach of all classes of the community. He was everyone's friend, as Cyril Noall emphasises in his history, *Smuggling in Cornwall*, as welcome with his surreptitious parcels and packages at the squire's hall and the rectory as at the labourer's cottage – his only enemies being the King's Men, officers of the Custom and Excise and their companions on the Revenue Cutters. Television viewers who watched Winston Graham's *Poldark* series will recall several episodes of daring coastal raids by smugglers, often running into ambushes laid by the wily Customs men.

Typically, like so much else in Cornwall, Cornish smuggling differed from that of most other parts of Britain. Elsewhere large vessels up to 300 tons were used and everything was highly organised by commercial groups – in Cornwall smuggling was very much an individual effort, using small cutters or fishing boats which would put into lonely coves along the Lizard Peninsula, or in Mount's Bay (where the name Prussia Cove commemorates the legendary exploits of John Carter, 'King of Prussia'). Needless to say the Cornish fishermen of their day were very much involved in smuggling, for their intimate knowledge of every inch of the tricky coastline, coupled with an inborn skill in handling fast sailing luggers, gave them an enormous advantage.

The dealings of the Cornish smugglers reached their height in the eighteenth century when 'Free Trade' had in fact acquired the status of a major industry. Boats from Roscoff in Brittany were landing their goods with impunity on the beaches, often being met by a welcoming crowd of fishermen and tinners. The goods would then be loaded on to the backs of ponies and donkeys (sometimes men, too). Of course there were frequent encounters with the vigilant customs men, but they were only human and open to bribes, thus the saying that they wore 'fog spectacles with bank note shades'! One way and another few smuggling runs failed, and few smugglers were caught, and for two or three centuries it was almost a routine business along wide open beaches such as Lelant or Hayle and Gwithian, on the north coast, or further up, Newquay, Padstow and Bude. On the south coast, at several spots along the huge sweep of Mount's Bay, and in particular the coastline from Polperro to Plymouth Sound, smuggling was carried out on a much bigger scale than anywhere else in Cornwall.

Cornish smugglers were not only daring, but ingenious – for a long time they even audaciously took their merchandise not merely into Falmouth Harbour, but right up the River Fal to St

Mawes and Tresillian Creek, and even into Truro itself, thirteen miles from the sea! Some idea of the scale of this river trade can be gauged from the fact that when a smuggler's packet boat was seized by the preventative officers just below Truro she was found to have on board 120 kegs of brandy.

As with other sea occupations, smuggling has not altogether passed into myth and legends by any means – every year one reads of instances of smugglers being caught in Falmouth and Fowey and the larger ports (nobody knows what may still be going on in smaller ports!) What has perhaps now superseded smuggling, and is of course a more law-abiding profession, is treasure-hunting. In recent years Cornwall has seen quite a boom in this, notably out in the Isles of Scilly, the most romantic venture there being the raising of the bullion from the wreck of Admiral Sir Cloudsley Shovell's *Association*, off the Gillstone Reef, an operation carried out by a team of divers led by Roland Morris, author of the fascinating *Island Treasure*.

Skin diving itself has opened up whole new worlds and insights in Cornwall, and for those who want to understand some of the mysteries of Cornwall and its sea then here, surely, may be the answer. Who knows? When diving off some craggy sea-swept rocks into the deep sea blue waters, you may swim down and down and encounter some strange whole hidden mysterious world, a lost land of Lyonesse indeed.

X

Land of Superstitions

Cornwall is a land full of superstitions and this is generally put down to their Celtic origin. It seems just as likely that the hazardous life style caused a belief in omens to develop and survive longer in our rather remote county than in more populated places. After all, mining and fishing are both dangerous occupations, the men being in constant peril from accidents or storms at sea, the women living always in the knowledge that some unlucky happening might deprive them all at once of their life's partner.

Be that as it may, over the years I have gathered together many examples of superstitions of all kinds. For instance sparrows twittering and rooks darting around their rookery are both signs of rain, as is the braying of a donkey. Hens must never be allowed to sit on an even number of eggs, eleven or thirteen being the luckiest numbers. Magpies invariably appear one at a time. The rhyme goes: 'One for sorrow, Two for joy, Three for a girl, Four for a boy, Five for silver, Six for gold, Seven for a secret that's never been told.' If you do see one on its own, there are two things you can do about it to avert the sorrow: either spit on your finger and make a cross on the toe of your shoe or take off your hat to it if you have one.

Crossing your shoe with saliva is also a cure for hiccoughs, but a cross must never be made underground or on the side of a mine. Never whistle when you are down there, either, or you will vex the 'knockers' – those small people who live down below ground, and who are inclined to be temperamental. Sing for them instead. If you are a miner and you meet a 'bullhorn' (snail) on your way to work, it is a good idea to drop down a wee bit of your dinner for him. Whistling does not seem to be a lucky thing to do, for sailors should not whistle on board ship, not talk about hares, either.

All those at sea must beware of annoying a mermaid or she may well decide to fill up your home harbour with sand. Fishermen know, of course, that they must always eat a pilchard from the tail up to the head, and they also know it is most unlucky for them to see a clergyman near the boats. Seamen, when ashore, will notice omens of coming storms, such as a cat frolicking around the house with 'the storm in its tail'. Animals and small children are very sensitive to windy weather, as any infant teacher knows; they tend to go a bit wild, and possibly a cat can feel the coming storm in advance.

Many of the old herbal cures were really helpful; 'quickenwood' carried in the pocket would ward off rheumatism. A man might contract this, apparently, by using a walking stick made of holly, but he could easily cure it if he found a bramble that had rooted twice and he crawled under the arch between. Many superstitions were concerned with being ill-wished, when people, and even cattle, were made ill, and sometimes they died, through the evil thoughts and sorcery of those who had a spite against them. Although innocent folks often suffered, this form of black magic has certainly been used, even recently, by tribes in Africa. Some sort of telepathy may be at the root of it.

Witches were very real to people a few centuries ago, and many harmless old men, as well as women, were tortured, just because they were odd and probably brewed concoctions of herbs. There were various ways of keeping witches from descending on their broomsticks near your house. You could plant an elder tree beside your door, hang up a horse-shoe (the right way up, of course, so that the luck could not run out) – or you could put out some 'hundreds and thousands'. This last remedy would keep the witch so busy counting them that she would have no time to come in! Small holed stones were hung up, too, often attached to a doorkey, as iron and stone combined to keep evil out, and pennies and pins always used to be dropped in wishing-wells.

Not only in Cornwall do people still dislike seeing the new moon for the first time through glass. Many people turn their money in their pockets as they look at this crescent in the sky and silently wish as they do so. In other areas, too, they say you will have seven years' bad luck if you break a mirror. Floating tea-leaves are called 'strangers', – you put them on your hand to smack them, and count the days, to find out when the strange visitor would appear. A hard tea-leaf foretold a visit from a man, but a soft one meant that a woman would arrive. (Robert Hunt said that flakes of smut on the firebars have the same meaning.)

Among other superstitions – it is always unlucky to pass someone on the stairs, and it is best to turn and go back rather than risk a quarrel. Itching and burning ears means that someone is thinking of you – 'right for spite and left for love', (though others say if the left one burns scandal is being talked about you, while burning of the right ear means you are being praised). Churchyards in Cornwall often have few or no graves on the north side of the church, where no sun could fall on those laid to rest. This side was supposed to belong to the devil and there is a little church in North Cornwall with a small opening in the wall to let the evil one go out through it during the baptism service. That is the only time the little aperture is opened.

There are many superstitions about the devil in Cornwall where the people seem particularly anxious to keep him away. Everyone west of Mount Misery, near Newlyn, was supposed to be safe, because his footprint is there, facing east, showing where he first landed in Cornwall. At Veryan there are round houses with no corners in which he could hide, and with a cross on top to make sure. Even so, he must have appeared in many places where his name is still found. His Letterbox, Bellows and Apron-strings can be seen at Kynance Cove, for instance; his Frying-pan at Grade; and his Jump in the little parish of Advent.

Various odd protections used to be taken against fire, one being the slough of an adder hung on the rafters. Tufts of dried seaweed were kept for the same reason on chimney pieces in fishermen's cottages as late as 1891. To rock an empty cradle means you will soon have another child to go in it, and a 'footling' (a baby born feet first) will certainly have magical powers. A dying person must have the bed the same way as the floor-boards run in order to die peacefully. The following unlucky things you must never do: Do not put a loaf upside-down on the table, or put shoes or bellow there; never cut the butter at both ends or spill the salt; be careful not to cross two knives or destroy a nest of ants; and a corpse must not be taken along a new road ... Many of these old superstitions linger on in Cornwall, and we still tend to believe in their magic omens.

I have been browsing through some of the old issues of the *Cornish Review* and it is surprising what a wide range of information can be gleaned about old customs, of which superstitions are a good example. Often we were able to recapture the feeling of old ways of life – as Muriel Sara did for us in her memories about 'the Bal Maidens':

'When I was a little girl I lived in Church Street, Camborne. It was such an interesting place to live, as there were always so many interesting things to watch from its windows – people going and coming out of church, weddings, funerals, listening to its lovely bells, playing hymn tunes. The German band would always come and play on Monday mornings outside the church. We would throw our pennies from the window to them. On Saturdays our street would be full of various stalls. All around the town were lovely country walks and places to visit, and thrilling things to do. One minute you would be in our busy street, and the next minute you would be out in a daisy-covered field, making daisy chains, fishing for tadpoles in pools, picking handsful of wild flowers, ferns, blackberries, nuts, according to the season.

'Camborne has grown so much that now you would have to walk further for nature's playground. We did not have any so-called Recreation Ground, nor did we need one. Among all the lovely walks that we would take was one to the North Cliffs. But we loved all the interesting things that we could do and see on our way there.

'We would go down our back lane, pass some very poor, tiny cottages, then be out in real lovely country now known as Wellington Road, lanes, fields and hedges. We would never walk on the flat if we could find a hedge possible to walk on. Some were very high, and rough, which made us feel as if we were on top of the world. We could watch all the cows, horses, ponies, donkeys and sheep in fields on each side of us. Until we came to a road which led to Tehidy, there was a very pretty house then known as Rosewarne Farm. The Bennett children lived there. They were school friends of ours. In front of the garden there was a lovely green splat, where little girls would gather with their dolls, for dolls' tea parties, and where, from a branch overhanging, the Bennett children had a swing. So sometimes we would stop and have a swing. What a pretty picture it would have made. Then we would turn to a pretty country road on the left and gather acorns, pass a white gate where a clever man named Mr Stephens lived. He often visited my parents and loved to speak of old Cornwall and his hope for its future. There had once been a strawberry garden there. You paid 6d. or 1/- and could pick as many as you liked. Then we would come to the most exciting bit – the tin stream – which collected waste tin from the mines before it was washed out to sea at Gwithian and Portreath.

'A Mr Stevens made a lot of money by collecting this waste, and lived in a house on the sands at Gwithian, very close to the sea. I went to school with his three daughters, Lilian, Flossie and Ethel, and would have loved to have lived on the sand by the sea. Those tin streams were rather like fields of red water and sand, with planks and wooden bridges, which led you over it at certain places. There were big break machines, which the "Bal Maidens" worked. Women of all ages, married, or mere girls, they were all known by that name. In the summer they wore cotton or print bonnets, big print sun bonnets, with an old sack used as an apron. In the winter they wore old coats and shawls, as it was very cold work. Their poor hands and feet would suffer much from chilblains and all.

'Among the Bal Maidens worked Aunt Harris. She was no relation of ours, but she was our Jane's aunt and her relations were always ours. (Her husband, I believe, had been killed in a mine accident.) We loved Aunt Harris, and always looked out for her and her rosy face and kind, dark eyes. She would allow us to cross over the damp red slippery bridges until we came to the bridge where she worked, and would show us how things were worked, and let us try and work the great brush, not so easy as it looked. We thought her very clever, and longed to be a Bal Maiden and wear a print bonnet. Sometimes there might be a big shower, or it was "crowse" time, then the "maidens" would gather in a long black shed and sit around a fire, drinking strong cups of tea out of terrible old cracked cups, almost as brown as their tea. Yet a sip out of one of these cups tasted nicer than tea at home, out of a spotless china cup.

'Often on Saturday afternoons we would visit Aunt Harris in her little cottage at Penponds, which was on the top of a bank. To get to it we would have to climb a lot of crooked little steps. We would usually find her in her garden shaking her mats; it was her only chance to clean her house, and she was very house-proud. She wanted to get her work done well and quickly, to get all dressed up to go to town to do her weekly shopping, and to meet the other Bal Maidens who had not gone for a walk with their miner sweethearts. So you would not think that she would welcome a pack of children; but you would always be sure of a smile and welcome from Aunt Harris.

'While she worked she allowed us to climb or pick apples from her old apple tree, when they were ripe (their colour was just like her weather-beaten cheeks), or play games in her garden. When it was wet or cold, she would allow us to admire her ornaments, and we thought them lovelier than mother's in our drawing-room at home. How we loved to hold and shake her little snowman under his glass dome!

'When the time came for us to go home, and say thankyou, we would go down the crooked little steps with a cheek puffed out with a bullseye, or a pocket full of apples, or a hand-full of gillyflowers (that is the old name for wallflowers) that she had picked for us to take home for mother, and Jane, her niece. We would return ever so hungry, and there was Jane in her best Saturday afternoon apron to greet us, and there was a smell of freshly-baked saffron buns, splits, seedy buns and heavy cake and on the table pound pats of golden butter that a farmer's wife had delivered fresh that afternoon (we always knew which, because of the cow or bunches of flowers printed on them), dishes of cream, jam, treacle or honey.

'After tea we would go up to our nursery and watch all the people in the street buying things from the various stalls, or stannions, as some people called them; cheap Jacks, or listen to the Town Crier, in his old high silk top buttoned hat. We looked out for Aunt Harris coming up to town, so that we could wave to each other. She always looked so smart, with a big feather in her hat, sent from South Africa by a mining relation of hers, her best high boots with patent leather toes. We were so proud that we had an Aunt Harris, and how smart she looked. You would never believe that she was a Bal Maiden.

'I feel quite sad for the many children of today. Life seems one mad rush to get somewhere and back again; they have missed all the lovely people, things by the way. How much they have missed!'

I went to see Muriel Sara once; she was a delightful old lady in her nineties who was still busy writing little sketches of this old way of life she remembered so vividly. When I think about it perhaps I should have called on more of our contributors for every one of them seemed to have an interesting story to tell, whether well known authors like Howard Spring or Leo Walmsley – or an old-fashioned clergyman, like Canon Miles Brown whose lovely church, St Minnow, stands on the banks of the River Fowey just above the village of Golant (about a mile or so from our old home at the Old Sawmills). It was Canon Brown who gave us this delightful portrait of a Cornish bell ringing practice.

'Take a walk up the hill with me on a Tuesday evening in winter, and you will discover a facet of village life which will enthrall you. For it is ringing-practice night at the parish church, and the local ringers enjoy a reverence for their skill among the members of the fraternity.

'Tall beech trees bend slightly in the wind, their lower main trunks lost in the shadows of the churchyard. The tower is faintly silhouetted against the night sky and an occasional owl hoots his displeasure at imminent disturbance of his nocturnal excursions. The gravel on the churchyard path crunches, and a coming torch casts shadows from the trees on the church wall, lighting now and then in its wavering course on the village tombstones. Jack, the captain, with his great tower-door key, fumbles for a while and then the oak door, studded with nails, swings open, letting out a whiff of that peculiarly Church-of-England odour, composed of dampness, candle smoke, scent of flowers, old hymn-books.

'A knot of shadowy figures detaches itself from among the trees and waits at the door. Jack finds the switch, and at once the light leaps out from open door and west window. Inside the church the walls and ceiling are criss-crossed with a pattern like a spider's web, of shadows thrown by the six bell-ropes, hanging in a circle, and gathered to hooks on the tower walls.

' "Evening Jack!" "Hullo Harry, all set for tonight, boy?" A few words of greeting, of market news, and farming talk. Then coats are taken off, and the ropes let fall into their circle.

"We'm but five," says Jack, and disappointment shows on the faces of the ringers. For five bells rung out of six leave much to be desired. "Where's Tom and Brice?" Then, as though in answer, comes a steady crunch of gravel, followed by the dot-and-carry-one tread of a limping man. Two more figures appear, taking off with simple reverence their caps as they enter the church tower. Practice can now begin, and a seventh man present means there can be a different manning of the ropes for better practice.

'The ropes with their bright "fillets" of red, white and blue and their long tails of plain rope are taken up, and the ends are gathered into coils in the hands of the ringers, who now stand, each by his bell, feet together, one hand on the fillet, the other with its coil just below.

'Jack, the captain, also rings the tenor, the largest bell. He is a tall, thin man who bends and unbends while ringing, suddenly, in the middle, like a footrule. This bodily rhythm helps him to ring steadily, he explains. Brice and the others take their usual places. Harry bites his moustache in anxiety, hoping to acquit himself well, for he is a comparative newcomer to the art, having taken it up only three years ago and with much to learn. Jim, on the treble, is a small, compact man with a pleasant face. He takes a quick competent look around at the team and there is a moment full of eager anticipation.

' "Look out, go," he calls. All six men bend to their ropes. For the first pull there is silence save for the creak of the great wheels of the bells high up in the tower darkness. Then, with a sudden dash of sound the six bells strike out in rapid and even order, gradually opening out as the bells are swung higher and higher towards the top of their upside-down balance. Back and forth they go, their wide bell-metal mouths rising to the sky, first on backstroke and then on handstroke, while with each tremendous tumble-over the iron clappers fly the width of the bell-mouth to send the music over farm and hamlet.

'Below in the ringing chamber the fillets soar higher and

higher as the bells rise, the ropes rattling in their guides and the ready hands catching them as they fall and rise. It looks so easy that it is hard to realise the skill needed to control exactly to the rhythm the half-ton or more of bell and clapper, wheel and stay. Each bell has its natural period, from the slow roll of the larger bells to the quick stroke of the smaller ones, but all must be held to the steady beat of the tenor.

' "Keep the second off on the end," says the captain. "Fourth's a bit wide on the fillet" – "Keep 'em to that! Now, look about it!"

'Tom, sitting with his back to the tower screen, has taken down from its nail in the wall, a board covered with figures, pair by pair. These are the changes to be called, for in our rural areas the sophistications of Grandsire Triples and Stedman Doubles are not. They may be all right for "they scientific chaps" of the town belfries, but here we "do belong" to call the changes one by one.

' "Second to third," says Tom over the rattle of ropes. In a moment the listener detects the order of striking has altered, the third bell sounding after the treble, and the second now after the third. Soon the original order of the descending scale is lost as the bells are called one to another. Only Jack, on the tenor, rings a mighty "full-stop" to each change, keeping his position as the last to sound.

'Some of the changes are more musical than others, and Tom pauses in his calling to let the flavour be savoured before announcing a further change. But soon the last ones are called, and the bells come home into rounds once more without a hitch, and "Up next Fillet" gives the command to rest the bells on their stays, the weight of bell-metal just held delicately upside down on the balance by a frail wooden bar.

'The echo dies away. The silence of the countryside takes over for a while as there is criticism of the peal just rung, advice to Harry, whose face glows with pride at a peal of changes rung without mistake. Then there is talk about the forthcoming ringing festival, for which all the local teams are practising hard, and hopes are expressed for a good placing in the competition.

'Tom now rises and takes his place by the third rope, looking expectantly at the captain, and soon the bells are swinging again in another peal. So the evening passes, till nine o'clock approaches. The single word "Downward," as the bells are smoothly in rounds brings a gradual quickening of the rhythm, the ropes are gathered in with a rapid turn of the wrist, and the swing of the bells gradually checked until they are gently oscillating with a quiet chime from each. A stamp from the boot, and all cease together and lapse into silence. There is a faint humming from the tower with the vibration of the great tenor bell, till even that fades away and the bells hang silent till Sunday morning sees them in play again.

'The ringers huddle on their coats, their faces shining with warmth and with pride of achievement. Their ancient art is being kept alive, the village tradition carried on. Young Harry, a modern in his facial hair, is "keeping it up" when so many of his generation lose interest in anything requiring patience and practice.

'There are farewells. Cars start up in the lane. The tower light goes off, the door slams, the key grates in the lock, the gravel crunches. Young Harry negotiates himself to the captain's side. "How did I do?" he asks nervously, for Jack is a stern critic. "Not bad," he says. This is high praise from him, and Harry beams in the darkness. His day has been made.

' " 'Night," and the last one has gone, leaving us alone with the sigh of the trees, the hoot of the returning owl, the small voices of the hedgerow.

'We walk back down the hill. Practice night is over.'

XI

The Towns of Cornwall

When I recently paid a rare visit to Cornwall's county town, Truro, and saw all the evidence of a newly thriving centre I realised that perhaps too often I have written about the sea-washed coastline of Cornwall. There is, after all, an inland Cornwall as well, and quite fascinating it can be, even some of the more industrialised centres like the St Austell area with its white tipped clay mountains, or Redruth or Camborne, or great lonely expanses like Bodmin Moor (rather than Bodmin town itself, which I always find rather lacking in character).

Truro is a different matter. Truro has considerable character. I well remember my old friend the painter Tom Early pointing out that here was a city which had not been treated justly, and how indeed most guide books passed it by as quickly as possible, referring to it with scarcely veiled contempt. In fact Truro is a city of surprises which is perhaps not surprising when one considers the length and importance of its history. In 1304 Truro was constituted a coinage town for tin, and remained an important centre for the metal during the next six hundred years – it was the meeting-place for a kind of tinners' trade union from early times. Even in 1911 it could be said that 'Truro has considerable trade in connection with the tin mines of the neighbourhood'. To-day little is left of this once proud industry except a few melancholy ruins on the surrounding hills. River traffic made it an important port, long before the upstart Falmouth; but bigger ships and the gradual silting up of the river have resulted in Falmouth taking its place. Now it is chiefly launches which run between the two towns, and so quickly does the tide come in that launches seem almost to follow in its wake. But I have seen coalers moored at the dockside which look absurdly large as they squat on the mud at low tide, though I don't suppose they were more than a few hundred tons. This stretch of river ought to be an artist's paradise, with its curving row of warehouses opposite, white and grey in the sun, and one strange building standing head and shoulders above the rest, coloured in the garish red of Victorian Gothic.

The usual view taken about Truro's Cathedral is 'that it might have been worse than it is – like the Law Courts in London, for example, which does not get us very far. Part of the old parish church has been skilfully incorporated into the building, and occasional glimpses of this seen down narrow streets give one the impression of an old cathedral town. But inside the ugly proportions and jaundiced colour of the stone do not add to that impression. However that may be, Tom Early used to recollect an occasion when a concert was given in the nave of the Cathedral by the BBC Symphony Orchestra, when the brass in Gabriele's Sonate sounded electrifying as the last rays of the sun came through the west window, and Brahm's Fourth Symphony achieved an unparalleled dignity. Outside there are many delightful Georgian houses built from the hard granite, yellow-grey in colour, or the softer, crumbling stone which seems to vary in colour from green and grey, through yellow, to orange and Lemon Street must be one of the finest in Cornwall.

And what of Truro people themselves? A recent writer has said that the memorial given to John Robarts of the seventeenth century, 'Reputed, grave, honest and very discreet', would fit Truro. Perhaps this is right, though I cannot see her reason for going on to say of the town that 'it leaves one cold', for there is a warmth, friendliness and vigour which makes nonsense of her words. Especially is this so on market day, when farmers come from far and wide to meet each other and to sell their pigs, cows, sheep, lambs, bulls and heifers and the auctioneer shouts against their background noise: 'Forty-forty-five – fifty – sixty – who'll bid sixty-two? – going at seventy – gone!' Off goes one heifer, and in comes another. So it goes on through the hot afternoon, until the Victoria Gardens no longer echo to the grunts, groans and cries. Certainly Truro has not produced men like Davy of Penzance or Trevithick of Camborne.

One man who left his mark was Samuel Foote the actor, reputed to have been born in the King's Head in 1720. A friend of Dr Johnson, Burke and Reynolds, he failed in both tragedy and comedy, and succeeded in running through two fortunes before he realised his power lay in mimicry.

Today Truro is a very modern and bustling city, even boasting a grand new Marks and Sparks, and with its huge County Hall edifice on top of the hill above the station it is truly the hub and centre of Cornish life. I think we have a county capital of which we can justly be proud.

What of some of the other Cornish towns? One with which I had a very close connection during the five years we lived at the Old Sawmills was Fowey, somewhat uniquely set on the side of a hill overlooking a lovely harbour with dozens of small boats, yachts, tugs and barges swinging at their moorings, not forgetting the ocean-going cargo boats that steam in for their loads of china clay. John Keast wrote us a very perceptive portrait of Fowey for the *Cornish Review*:

'I can think of no finer place to settle to write about Fowey than a seat at the end of Hall Walk. To reach this you must cross the river from Passage Slip, remembering that this Ferry is one of the oldest in Cornwall: a chart of the harbour drawn about 1540 includes a tiny sketch of the Bodinnick ferry boat of that time and records show that the Passage was in use long before then. Having climbed the prodigiously steep Bodinnick Hill it is advisable to rest against the hedge for a few minutes and draw breath before stepping out through a copse of tall trees to the Walk beyond. Here you will find Carew's description, written in the reign of Queen Elizabeth, holds good today and that: –

> your eyes shall be called away from guiding your feet to descry by their farthest kenning the vast Ocean sparkled with ships that continually this way trade, forth and back, to most quarters of the world. Nearer home they take view of all sized barges and fisher boats hovering on the coast. Again contracting your sight to a more narrower scope, it lighteth on the fair and commodious haven, where the tide daily presenteth his double service of flowing and ebbing, to carry and re-carry whosoever the Inhabitants shall be pleased to charge him withall and his creeks (like a wanton lover) fold about the land with many embracing arms.

'The vantage point is reached some fifty yards this side of the granite obelisk which was erected in 1948 to commemorate "Q" (who also loved this spot and rowed across from "The Haven" to spend many pleasant hours in his garden below this Walk). Here you may enjoy the broad panorama – the "fair and commodious haven" to the left with small boats, yachts, harbour tugs and barges swinging at their moorings, the river so admirably described in a recent book, below and to the right of the scene. On the far side of the river the town ascends the hillside, first the rough harbour walls, sea-weed clinging to their base and red valerian to their upper levels, then the houses rising in terraces, roof upon roof, all in delightful miniature. Indeed, one of the joys of this view is the feeling it gives you of being another Gulliver looking down upon the house-tops of a Cornish Lilliput.

'There are actually three parts to the town, each visibly defined – the ancient grey walled houses and quays, with here and there touches of pink and green wash, stretching in a broken line along the water's edge to just beyond the Town Quay, the villas, hotels and boarding houses extending almost to St Catherine's Point, and the new suburb, windows glinting in the sunlight, which crowns the hill top.

'For a place of its size – it has a population of barely two thousand – Fowey is an example of "multum-in-parvo" with maritime activity as the theme. It is a commercial port and a port of registry for sea-going vessels. Around a bend in the river, judicially separated from the town by Caffa Mill Pill, are a number of electrically equipped jetties capable of dealing with the bulk of the china clay which is exported from Cornwall to the Potteries, America and the Continent. During the last sixty years there has been a change in the size and type of vessel using the port. In the 1920's large British, American and Japanese freighters and a multitude of small tramp steamers of various nationalities, with a sprinkling of schooners and barquentines loaded here. For days at a stretch these vessels would lie in tiers at their moorings in the river awaiting their turn to come alongside and, as in the Middle Ages, at intervals Fowey seemed almost cosmopolitan. Occasionally ocean-going sailing ships called and I remember the sight of the Finnish barques *Elakoon* and *Varma*, sister ships painted white above the water-line, with trim varnished yards, lying below Hall Walk waiting for a favourable wind to take them down Channel.

'As a holiday resort Fowey has changed since the day Richard Jefferies preferred to go to Penzance rather than be shut in Fowey. Miss Sarah Jukes was the first person to live to the westwards of Whitehouse and she died in 1871. From 1880 onwards considerable efforts were made to establish Fowey in the ranks of the lesser holiday resorts. The Yacht Club was formed, a little golf course laid out on the cliffs and a number of hotels and boarding houses were built on the seaward side of the town. The old Ropewalk, redundant when sailing ships gave way to tramp steamers and wire hawsers to a great extent superseded manilla, hemp and coir, was taken over for building purposes and renamed the Esplanade. In our time the Borough Council has assumed responsibility for extending amenities and the Town Quay, Whitehouse and Readymoney beaches have been greatly improved.

'A few years ago it was proposed to construct a promenade from the Broad Slip to the Town Quay and to demolish many of the intervening houses and shops. Fortunately the scheme, which would have drastically changed the appearance of the Fore Street, never came to anything. Our Fore Street has a character of its own. At one end the glassy eye of the old Custom House squints down the whole narrow length of the street – past the Broad Slip, where Queen Victoria and the Prince Consort landed in 1846 and the "Noah's Ark" that picturesque structure which is the remaining part of what was probably the residence of a prosperous merchant in Tudor times to the "Lugger" which conceals a seventeenth century house behind a modern frontage. Visitors are occasionally disappointed to find so few gabled "Elizabethan" houses in Fowey. The truth is that until a hundred years ago the town was confined to a relatively small area bounded by the North and South Gates and the ancient architecture – mediaeval rather than "Elizabethan" – has been hidden from sight by periodical attempts to renovate old buildings rather than pull them down. Many houses which today present a frontage of cement wash or brick have the old rough Cornish cob only a few inches below the surface.

'Around from the Fore Street the size and magnificent proportions of St Fimbarrus Church provide some evidence of the importance of Fowey six hundred years ago when it ranked with Plymouth and Southampton and had a great trade in tin, wool, wine and fish. Behind the church is Place, the earliest part Tudor and the more recent completed just a century ago. In any other setting this castellated mansion might seem a little incongruous but here it blends with the ancient church and the white-washed cottages at Cobbs Well and gives added dignity to the town.

'On Saturday afternoons in the summer, visitors and local inhabitants line the margin of the Town Quay to watch racing between yachts of the Troy class. The Yacht Club, of which "Q" was for many years Commodore occupies a corner of Whitford's Yard close to where the last vessel to be built at Fowey was launched in 1878. Annual events such as the Yacht Club regatta and the Dockers' regatta attract a number of spectators and formerly light, four-oared boats – the "Sport", "Docker", "Defender" and others – were specially built to uphold the honour of Fowey, Polruan and places as far afield as Charlestown and Looe. A carnival procession usually followed on Town regatta days but in recent years the imported "Furry Dance" led by the Town Crier (once again Champion Crier of England, Scotland and Wales) in his blue and red robes and cocked hat, has found favour and it must be admitted that the narrow winding main street is admirably suited for the performance.

'So much for the lower town. In the years following the first World War an enterprising builder started to erect houses on the high ground near Lawhyre farm. Reached by a stiff climb up Lostwithiel Street and New Road Hill this suburb of Fowey has grown considerably and is now made up partly of Council Houses and partly of privately owned dwellings. Lately a number of Cornish Unit houses have made their appearance and wartime Admiralty huts have been converted into temporary homes.

'It is unfortunate that many visitors arriving by car, pass through this outgrowth of Fowey, pleasantly and healthily situated but as yet possessing no specific character of its own, drive down the steep hill to the Town Quay, get out and stare about the harbour for a brief interval and then set off by the same route as they came, bearing away the impression that there is really nothing much to see at Fowey. To enjoy our town properly you must stay awhile, explore the old alleys and courts, take out a boat and pull up the river early in the morning when the mists are just rising from the water or tramp among the bramble and bracken along the edge of Colvethick Wood.'

Redruth is one of the great industrial towns of Cornwall, and one of the best portraits of it was that we published in the *Review* by the historian, the late Frank Michell, who declared his intention of taking a stand upon four platforms in turn:

'The great granite mass of Carn Brea is our first step. This was the birthplace of the town, and it has ever been its background and landmark. Much has been written about this hill both of a fanciful and scientific nature. There is ample evidence of man's habitation of Carn Brea from the remains of Stone Age huts and relics of this period, and also of the Bronze Age, which have been discovered on its heights. A Roman urn and coins of various rulers of that Empire have been found on the Carn, and also a coin of a North African kingdom of 148 BC. A granite stone set up by the Romans, AD 224-244, may be seen near Gwennap Pit just south-east of Redruth. Tradition tells us that woodcock once abounded in the valley from the foot of Carn Brea to the north coast, and that there were trees from the hill to Portreath, so that a squirrel could travel from the Carn to the sea without touching ground. The castle was probably never really used as a fortress, and it is sited a little east of the place of an ancient defensive earthwork. Davies Gilbert, writing in 1820, says that the castle was built by the Bassets as an ornament to their deer park. As far back as 1379 a licence was granted to the Bassets to hold a service in their chapel on Carn Brea. The monument nearby was raised in 1836 to the memory of Lord De Dunstanville and Basset, it is 90 feet high, stands 750 feet above sea level, and cost £1,000 to erect.

'We mount to the second step, the ecclesiastical story. About AD 550, half a century before the time of St Augustine of Canterbury, St Euny came from Ireland to Lelant and thence to Redruth. He made contact with the primitive tribes of Carn Brea, taught them Christianity and built himself a cell, probably on the eastern slope of the hill. His holy well was in the valley below (the place may still be visited), and he built his oratory on or about the site of the present parish church. The times gradually became more settled and civilized, and the natives descended from the hills to the greater space of the valleys and surrounding country. The population increased with greater security. St Euny's little chapel was probably followed by a rude Saxon type building and later by a Norman church, the foundations of which, showing an apse, were exposed in 1878 beneath the present church floor. The earliest mention of the church fabric occurs in 1283, and the oldest known spelling of its name, and that of the parish, is found in 1316, when it was styled "Sancti Eunyny de Rudruthe". In 1400 a licence was granted to the rector for a chapel of St Rumon, Cross Street. This was probably a shrine and resting-place for pilgrims passing through the town to St Michael's Mount, and built on or about the site occupied to-day by Murdock House and where a few remains may be seen. This grant also provided for a chapel to St Christopher (site unknown) and a deed of 1513 shows that there was another chapel, dedicated to St Ninian, at Sinns in the ancient parish on the road from Redruth to Porthtowan.

'On four occasions between 1411 and 1419 Bishop Stafford of Exeter held ordinations (for minor orders) at Redruth which, for this purpose at least, seems to have been a centre and a place of some importance. About 1495 the parish church was rebuilt – only the fine perpendicular tower of which remains today. This tower contains eight bells dating from 1744, 1777 and 1935 (change ringing was reintroduced in 1912 "for the first time in living memory"), and on its eastern wall are carved the heads of Henry VII and his queen. A Norman gargoyle may be seen in the angle of the nave with tower. In 1768 the present church was, in the words of Davies Gilbert, "constructed on the exact situation of the former". The three roofs are concealed by a coffered ceiling supported on eight Tuscan columns, four on each side.

'Many additions and improvements of good local workmanship have been made to the furnishing. Within the church are memorial tablets to S.V. Pryce, 1817 (son of Dr

William Pryce, of Redruth, who published *Mineralogia Cornubiensis*, etc.) and William Davey, 1827, who did much to improve methods of mining and the lot of the miners – his likeness here was sculpted by Chantry. There is also a portion of the ancient Celtic parish preaching cross, worked stones of the fifteenth century fabric and a medieval leaden crucifix which was dug up in the churchyard. The church Sunday School was established at the early date of 1780. From 1277 until 1916 the Basset family held the patronage. The modern church of St Andrew is built on or about the site of the old Treruffe Manor House.

'John Wesley visited Redruth many times between 1745 and 1789. He was a friend of the Rev John Collins, MA, Rector 1734-1775. At the time of Wesley's last visit he writes in his *Journal* of meeting the Methodist Society in the town and in the 1796-7 Church Rate the Methodist stewards are mentioned, and by 1803 there is a rate on the Methodist preacher's house. The present Wesleyan chapel dates from 1826, and there was at least one earlier on or about the same site. The Baptist Society in the town was established in 1802 and the Society of Friends in 1763. Most other religious bodies have subsequently had representation in Redruth.

'The third step in painting the portrait is copper and tin. Redruth has been one of the great mining areas of the world, and the industry is immemorial, for Cornish "mining" existed before English history. Legend has it that St Paul came to Creegbraws, near Redruth, for tin. Ryd, later Rys or Res, means a "ford" and Ruth, pronounced "Reeth", means "red". The Red River which reached the sea at Portreath (Red Cove or, perhaps, Sand Cove) derived its name and blood-red colour from the tin streaming industry which it served for centuries and which was well established by 1301.

'After Queen Elizabeth's time shallow-shaft mining, which had commenced in a small way about a hundred years before, gradually developed. Toward the end of the seventeenth century there sprang up extensive copper mining ventures around Redruth. Due to the introduction of the steam engine there was much industrial prosperity, and the population of the town increased sixfold during the century, being about 6,000 by the year 1800. During the nineteenth century the mining for tin followed that for copper, and the population eventually rose to its peak of 10, 685 in 1871. In 1838 there were employed in twenty-nine mines in the Redruth district, 6,886 men, women and children, and copper ore was sold to the value of £315,728. It has been estimated that there are sixty-six abandoned workings in the parish.

'To complete the sketch, and it is but a sketch for the subject matter is almost without limit, we stand on the last step – the town of Redruth. It is a mile by the direct route of the Church Lanes from the ancient church town. It came into being some time before the fourteenth century, around a ford on the stream flowing to Portreath, which was here crossed by a very ancient road. The Cornish word for tribe or clan is "trev", and in Redruth there have never been more or less than six treves – Treleigh, Treruffe, Trefula, east of the stream; Trewirgie, Trewingey and Trengweath to the west. The town grew up and became a centre at the meeting-place of five treves near the spot where the main track crossed the stream. The Church-town remained a hamlet apart while another village developed to the north beyond the Green. This latter was Plain-an-gwarry – the place of the play – where stood the open-air theatre or round for miracle plays, etc. When visited by Borlase in 1792, it remained a mound "high but ruinous". The town developed but little south of the main road (Fore Street) and the parallel street (Back Lane West and East, which may well have the original track over the ford which was adjacent to St Rumon's Chapel).

'The long narrow main street had buildings in the middle and numbers of courts leading off on either side. There are records of the visitations of plague in 1592 (84 deaths in an estimated population of 400) and in 1667, and of cholera and smallpox in 1849-50 and 1853. Considerable building took place during William III and Queen Anne's reign. The first clock tower built, about the end of the seventeenth century, gave place to a second, which with the market place, was demolished in 1795, and was replaced by the present clock in 1828, which was heightened in 1904. The present Market House was built in 1877. The eighteenth and nineteenth century building was first to the north and largely following the construction of the railway across the town in 1852, to the south of the main street.

'Redruth has for at least two and a half centuries been an industrial and commercial community, and its "cultural" activities have sprung largely from men engaged in these pursuits. Space permits us only to list some of the outstanding citizens who have not already been mentioned (for many the town was their birthplace). Fourteenth century: Sir Davis Aunselm, Rector, made the best copy of Edward I's valuation of English churches; Ralph Redruth (or Rudryth) became Chancellor of Oxford University. Fifteenth century: Reginald Mertherderwa, Rector, became Principal of Bull Hall (Merton), Oxford, and willed to be buried in Christ Church. Eighteenth century: Stephen and Anthony Cock of the Tinner's Parliament (they issued farthing tokens locally); William Churchill, High Sheriff; William Bull, Jonathan Hornblower and Michael Loam, engineers (they lived nearby and Redruth was their post town); William Murdoch (he married a Redruth girl); Dr William Boase, surgeon, who helped Murdoch in his experiments and also led a split off Methodism; James Watt; Richard Revithick (his mother was a Redruth girl); John Holman and Richard Scantlebury, machinery experimentalists; R.E. Raspe, author; Richard Hampton, itinerant preacher (whose biography was published). Nineteenth century: George and Richard Tangye, engineers; J.T. Blight, author and illustrator; Dr Robert Hunt, mining professor and educationalist; Madam Fanny Moody, singer of international fame; R.H. Heath, composer and publisher of Cornish carols, etc.: T.C. Peter, antiquarian and historian and author;

Passmore Edwards. In this century, Philip Snowden, later Chancellor of the Exchequer, and Canon G.H. Doble, D.D.'

As a complete contrast to Redruth one might well take Cornwall's 'Blackpool', the seaside town of Newquay. To those who know Newquay there are two towns, the real, which is mainly the progeny of the fertile inbreeding of hotels, struggling and jostling and developing in ribbons, contending with violent growth of wings and windows for each inch of sea view, and the Newquay that might have been. This is a planner's dream, and few of this kind seem to come to reality nowadays. Perhaps in this remote place, had some visionary realized its possibilities in time, the justification of all planners might have arisen. Almost a mile behind the unmatched coastline and beaches, a green and golden belt never to feel the impact of brick, in the Trenance valley there might have been a town that in setting of sublimity might have contended with the world. But real towns do not begin like this, and Newquay, as Carew suggests, had its rather dim origins in the coastal trade and in pilchard fishing.

There are few pilchards caught nowadays. Once, and much less than a century ago, there were pilchard cellars in many nooks around the harbour, and even now shelters and perhaps boathouses are still called locally by the names of the pilchard boats, *Fly, Good Intent* and *Active*. These names are still to be seen upon some of the Ordnance Survey maps. The older part of the town, that has somehow preserved its integrity, breathes faintly in the narrower streets a suggestion of former days.

The harbour is as it was, and in some of the houses in Fore Street it is possible on summer afternoons when the doors are open to look through to the blue sea beyond. There are prints of sailing ships in those small rooms, and one remembers a tea party on the balcony above the harbour, a retired skipper as host, splits and cream, and a white, tame herring-gull that came close nervously and beaked up the fragments. There were more real seafarers in the town even ten years ago, they still pottered in boats in the harbour, and recalled the days of sail.

The only coastal trade now is in holiday-makers, an hour round the bay; this sea is formidable enough for any visiting stomachs to realize that Cornish tripping on the north coast is different. When it really blows, and this is frequently, it is necessary to remain in the harbour.

One of the predominant memories of Cornwall to one who has grown up there as John Hewish once wrote in the *Cornish Review* is the glimpse that is the centre of a nebula of emotion, the sloping road and small stone houses, that frame blue water. Newquay has many of these saving glimpses, especially in the older part of the town, in Bank Street and East Street and in the roads about the harbour. A terrace here and a lane there, not worthy of notice in themselves, yield a sudden picture, and one says, 'How Cornish!' The sea absorbs and reflects, giving individuality to what would be quite featureless.

Newquay is mentioned in the earlier books upon Cornwall as being formerly called Towan. The beach nearest to the centre of the town derives its name from this, which means in the original language an area of blown sand, and the locality must have consisted in early days of such a region, and the present beautiful golf links remain to suggest its nature. Tales are still told of how the inhabitants tore up the foundations of one of the large outlying hotels; the space was used for drying nets, and some modern planners might have approved, though for a different reason. Newquay in ancient times was only a village in the parish of St Columb Minor, with no church of its own. The present large parish church was intended for a rapidly expanding town. Coastal coal and pilchards have been replaced as industries by the holiday-makers, and Towan Beach looks like a local Coney Island in August.

Beaches are the feature for which Newquay is memorable, long shining beaches that extend in every direction. North to Watergate and Mawgan Porth and westward to Perranporth. They are illimitable in variety and charm. Fistral, with its splendid sweep and awe-inspiring surf, Tolcarne, Great Western, and crowded Towan. They seem to get even finer as one moves away from the town. Even in the height of the season there is room for solitude, if one is prepared to walk or bus for a short distance, and for the more ambitious there are solitary bays waiting to be taken possession of for a season, and that the minds of children can possess like a Paradise. There is surely nothing like this in England. Above Padstow and Trevose the coast is less friendly, the cliffs offer nothing but the sea, and shelters like Port Isaac exist by the sufferance of Nature only. And southward there is only St Agnes and the darker beaches of the Perran tin lode. The strength of the surf and the character of the cliffs together have created the Newquay beaches. On the north coast the sunshine falls principally from behind to illuminate the sea, thus there is a scientific reason for the colouring that is the charm of North Cornwall. The cliffs themselves are variegated and are mosaics of abstract pattern and subtle colouring where the sun strikes, especially in the more horizontal lighting of winter. Entering the town by the main road in the evening, the bays and headlands extend in the distance almost to St Agnes beacon. The headlands are similar in shape, Towan, Pentire and West Pentire and each of the latter have detached rocks to seaward, called the Goose and Chick.

The environs of Newquay give the locality a flavour that the town itself lacks, with the deep and lochlike tranquillity of the Gannel estuary at full tide, where the sea at spring tides enters so swiftly. This estuary and the bay of Crantock, with its fierce surf, take on a unique melancholy in the late summer and autumn, with the brown headland slopes and the wide and deserted beach. Crantock and West Pentire are pervaded with the noise of the surf, it becomes a part of the walls of cottages and of lanes and hedgerows near the sea.

It is not so difficult, then, to believe the stories that were current in the Newquay of fifty years ago, of the dreadful screams of the Gannel Crake that, according to different versions of the tale, drove the listener mad or presaged a death at sea. Not so different either to hear the bells of the lost city beneath the Perran sands. It is strange how this seems to be one of the perennial legends, occurring in many places. It suggests comparison with the Lyonesse story or the legend of Debussy's *Cathedrale Engloutie*. The oratory of St Piran did appear strangely from the sands in the last century, and visiting it is one of the popular long walks from Newquay. St Carantoc figures slightly in Cornish Arthuriana. On one farm shed in Crantock the figurehead from a wreck may be seen. It is now the lintel of a doorway, and the cob wall presses deathlike on the wooden breasts.

Going in the northward direction there is the impressive and narrow bay of Porth, once a port, and where traces of the submarine forest still appear on the beach. In the cliffs of Porth Headland are huge caverns, only to be reached at low tide, and where one remembers the pre-war concert parties by candlelight. Beyond is bay after bay – Watergate, where the sands extend for miles, and Mawgan Porth, narrow and frowned upon by cliffs.

A portrait should perhaps show in its delineation the passage of time. For those who can remember the earlier days, it is evident that Newquay has not improved, except in size. The hotels may extend, but do not become more beautiful. The ugly tetter of hoardings and the cult of the snack bar, and the blue gigantic dance hall, are evident. One notices with regret the enclosure of even more land on lovely Pentire for building. Nobody knows better than a Cornishman the magic of a seascape enframed in his own window, but the price of his sea view is sometimes heavy in the currency of the spirit. Hotels are worth much, and this is evident to the native, who has watched some of the best of his locality disappear. These reflections are strangely necessary in an age that conceives apparently unrealizable dreams of green belts and preserved headlands. In the winter, Newquay hotels are illuminated briefly at Christmas, and the town is more Cornish and tranquil. Crowds gather in the Central Square in Saturday gloaming to discuss football results, and one might, listening to the talk, be in any country town, in Bodmin or Truro. The red eye of Trevose Light winks across the bay, and the noise of the surf is more noticeable in the quiet evening.

This was how John Hewish summed up his native town:

'During the extent of the season the town takes on the function for which it has refreshed itself in winter. The beaches fill alternately with tides and holiday-makers. There is nowhere, except perhaps Perranporth, where the surf-riding is so good as on Fistral beach. After a hot day the sea at Towan beach may be entered, as inviting and warm as milk. Rock pools contain fish with big heads, blennies and prawns, and the reflected faces of children. Headlands and sunbathers brown together. The old Huer's House on Towan headland, where the herald of the pilchard shoals blew his horn, is now climbed to give a fine view of the circle of bays. Building extensions on the way to St Columb Minor, once a pleasant walk through fields, take on a more genial character in the sunshine, almost Mediterranean. The sea glitters in all the peeps from the town. There are few trees in North Cornwall, and the seaward side of Newquay is especially bare of the palms that give a different atmosphere to Falmouth and Penzance. Sunshine is necessary to its individuality.

'Newquay remains a varied, straggling, but still lovable locality, fanatically upheld by those who know it, with the turbulence of Cornwall's worst or best resort, depending upon the point of view. Busy in summer as quiet as the deserted lounge of an hotel in the winter months, and not easily dismissed from the minds of those who remember an August on Fistral beach or a winter's afternoon on the headlands of Holywell or Bedruthan.'

Yes, Cornwall's towns have many and varied qualities – like our own 'local', Penzance, a pleasing mixture of market town and holiday centre. St Ives, Hayle, Camborne, Helston, Falmouth, Looe, Liskeard, Wadebridge, Bude, Lostwithiel ... you can take your pick, and always find something of interest.

XII

New Houses and Old

When our daughter Gill and her husband Alan finally acquired Tresidder Mill, the property adjoining our home in the valley, they were fulfilling a dream which like all dreams often threatened to turn into something of a nightmare. Certainly in those first few months there were problems – but then there had been problems galore during the previous two years or so of on and off negotiations with the previous owner, Sheila Ley. Sheila always liked Gill and Alan and wanted them to have the house, but they for their part kept hesitating. What helped to make up their minds in the end was an unexpected and rather threatening development – we learned that someone else was after the property, someone we all knew and thoroughly disliked. The prospect of this person as a close neighbour was more than any of us could bear, let alone Gill and Alan. We held a family gathering.

'You simply must get the place,' said Jess firmly. 'Then the valley will belong to the family altogether.' She paused and then added rather melodramatically. 'Otherwise ... '

Gill and Alan looked unhappy.

'The trouble is we don't think we can quite manage it ... '

'Well, perhaps we can all help a little.'

In the end the deal went through – and in the process there came into existence a strange new body we called GROT, consisting of various members of the family whose mission in life was to offer advice to Gill and Alan on how to develop their new property. For instance, what about developing the land – all those paddocks and fields. Maybe some market gardening? And horses, did they want to keep horses? There were some old stables that would suit. Then there was the old mill in the garden – wouldn't that be worth renovating?

Before I go further in this little saga I should quote from some sales details which gives a clearer picture of Sheila Ley's old home:

Tresidder Mill

Approached by a lane leading off the road from St Buryan via Crean to Polgigga, Tresidder Mill, set in a lovely and secluded valley about 2 miles from Land's End, is an interesting and unusual property comprising a main house, a converted mill and numerous other outbuildings, together with some $3\frac{1}{2}$ acres of land including sub tropical gardens, paddocks, fruit trees and woods. The main residence, all on one floor, consists of a lounge, 16 by 13 ft, a kitchen-breakfast room 13 by 8 ft, a dining room, $11\frac{3}{4}$ by 10 ft, a bedroom $11\frac{3}{4}$ x $10\frac{1}{2}$ ft, a second bedroom $8\frac{1}{2}$ x $7\frac{1}{2}$ ft, a third bedroom 8 x $7\frac{1}{2}$ ft and a bathroom and toilet. Cooking and water heating by oil-fired stove, and there is mains electricity, well water by electric pump, septic tank drainage and telephone. Nearby is a mill comprising a large central room 16 by 12 ft, together with small bathroom and bedroom. Among the out-buildings are a greenhouse, stables, stores, workshop, garage, etc. The paddocks are in fact large fields running down to the River Penberth. An outstanding feature is a trout stream and bridge just opposite the house front porch. Altogether the property offers immense possibilities either as a family home, or for holidays, or for riding, market gardening, etc. Although secluded, reached by a private lane, the property is close to several beautiful beaches – Porthcurno, Porthgwarra, Nanjizel and Sennen Cove – as well as the famous Minack Open Air Theatre. An excellent primary school is within easy walking distance and there are shops at Polgigga, Porthcurno and St Buryan (2 miles). The busy market town of Penzance is 8 miles distance – also within easy reach are Lamorna, Mousehole, Newlyn and St Ives. A property such as Tresidder Mill, in the heart of lovely West Cornwall, offers an unusual opportunity to anyone seeking a home in a beautiful and secluded setting.

Like our own home, Tresidder Mill was very ancient (it had of course originally been part of one single property occupying the whole valley). Just how ancient both properties were we had never quite realised until, while doing some research at the Penzance Library, our friend Frank Ruhmrund came across some fascinating biographical details. Apparently our home and Tresidder Mill, then all one property, had originally been built as far back as 1213! Frank found a record of the manor of Tresidder being held in that year by one Pharamus de Walesborough who left a widow with the rather marvellous name of Osmunda, and she claimed one third as a 'dowry'. It was also recorded that an ancestor Roger de Walesborough had once made a pilgrimage to the Holy Land and returned with a fragment of the Holy Cross which at one time was encased in a silver reliquary and deposited in St Buryan Church. Perhaps later it had been hidden somewhere at Tresidder? Who knew – for a time we all went round searching hopefully.

Among other news found by Frank was a record that our Mill House had been built with beams which were from shipwrecks at nearby Penberth and Porthcurno – also that one of the inhabitants early in the century had been Alexander Gibson, son of John Gibson of the Isles of Scilly. Alexander had quarrelled with his father so came over to the mainland and lived for some years at the Mill House.

Later the Mill House was held by the Spencer brothers for the cultivation of pedigree bulbs. Incidentally Frank's researches showed that at one time there were two mills, ours and the smaller one in Sheila Ley's gardens. The leat ran along the bank to the east of the valley and the iron arch in Sheila's garden with rectangular holes was the pit wheel of the mill and drove one pair of stones. Apparently our mill ceased to work as a flour mill some time before 1923, and after that was simply used for the generation of electricity – at least until 1947 when the wheel collapsed in the very bitter frost of that bad winter.

In his researches Frank uncovered many references to the beautiful gardens at Tresidder Mill, and how in 1958 the then owner, John D. Chilvers, 'by dint of great labour and almost entirely by hand had restored the grounds to a beautiful garden – trout in the mill pond being so tame that they come to feed from crumbs thrown to them'. Later the Leys took over, while of course prior to our coming the Mill House had been occupied for more than thirty years by Gladys and Sam Main, both keen supporters of the Minack Theatre (Gladys working making costumes and properties for the West Cornwall Theatre Group for many years).

So much for history, back to the present. The sale of Tresidder Mill had finally gone through, now the time had come for action. Several excited meetings of GROT were held and at the end of it all Gill and Alan decided they would (a) repair the roof of their new bungalow, (b) renovate the old mill in the garden, and (c) start exploring the possibilities of market gardening, riding, etc.

Renovating the mill proved an interesting experience. The main heavy work was done by Alan and Stephen, but Gill and Jess and Genevieve all contributed their quota of scraping and painting. Much of the mill was badly overgrown, but once it had been uncovered all kinds of possibilities were opened up. Suddenly where there had been darkness there was light – a comfortable place for putting up guests, or maybe a ready made studio for Alan to replace the rather small one he was using at the moment.

Either way the possibilities were exciting. Indeed during the whole of that spring and summer it often seemed that we spent as much time over at Tresidder Mill as we did at our own Mill House. It was, after all, fun to have new grounds to walk through – thick woods to be explored (in the middle a little summer house known as a gazebo), wide paddocks to be toured – and everywhere water, the gurgling stream continuing its wanderings around our own garden. Tresidder Mill had one great asset we lacked – a proper trout pool absolutely teeming with trout, and we spent hours sitting on the bank watching the little brown and silver creatures darting about.

Soon Gill and Jess went to work decorating the bungalow, while Alan and Stephen retiled the roof. The latter job was soon done but the decorating and furnishing went on for many weeks – I think Jess got quite a kick out of taking part, even though it wasn't her house. By the time the girls had finished, and Alan and Stephen had given the outside a new coating of paint, the bungalow was all shining and bright, like new.

'Soon be time for a house warming party,' we said hopefully.

Meantime things had not exactly been standing still over at the Mill House, where Jess steadily pursued her dream of a patio outside the kitchen. After making inquiries Stephen hired a JCB and spent two ferocious days tearing up the ground, heaving great boulders of granite this way and that. The carnage was terrible, everything looked like a gigantic battlefield. Still at the end of it all the ground had been levelled out all ready for the next stage – paving slabs and gravel. Here we had a stroke of luck, the Cornwall County Council were selling off some paving slabs cheaply, so we acquired thirty of these and then ordered several tons of sand.

It all took time, and as ever there were unexpected problems. Our worst one was a lump of granite so big that not even the JCB had been able to move it – in the end, however, we accomplished our levelling out intent by calling in an old Newlyn quarryman who brought along his special tools and with consummate skill managed to split and trim the granite boulder until it was down to the required size.

Working around Gill and Alan's new home, and then

writing about it all, made me wonder not for the first time whether I was justified in using our family life as 'material'. But then, as if to make the answer clear for me, there arrived in the post the following letter, from Southampton:

Dear Mr Val Baker,

Before I start my letter I think it only fair to warn you that it is of the 'I've read all your books' type, so if you've something better to do, now is the time to put this in the bin and go! It has taken me nearly two years to trace all the books in your family biographies and conversely my last one was your first, *The Sea's in the Kitchen*. This volume was run to earth by my local library service to the mobile library somewhere down the leafy lanes of Alton in the north of Hampshire. All I really want to say is thank you very much and to let you know how much I thoroughly enjoyed reading them all. You've helped enrich a love of Cornwall which was already strong, made me stop and think of certain attitudes of mine, and at times made me heartily disagree with you. I've always felt that a lot of the appeal of autobiographies, is contained in the 'peering thro' the window' idea, but you've always managed to prise open the door and there has never been any sense of invasion. Once again many thanks for many hours of reading. Before I finish, I hope you'll forgive me mentioning the recent *Forty minutes* programme in which you and your family featured. Any pre-conceived ideas I had before the showing were swept away by the sense of warmth and love that the film put over. Good luck, good health and peace to you and all your family.

Regards
Rod Andrew

After receiving such a nice fan letter I felt able to relax. Yes, it was all right to write about our family life for obviously it gave real pleasure to readers. But how nice of Mr Andrew to take the trouble to write – peace to you, too, Mr Andrew.

And now – back to work!